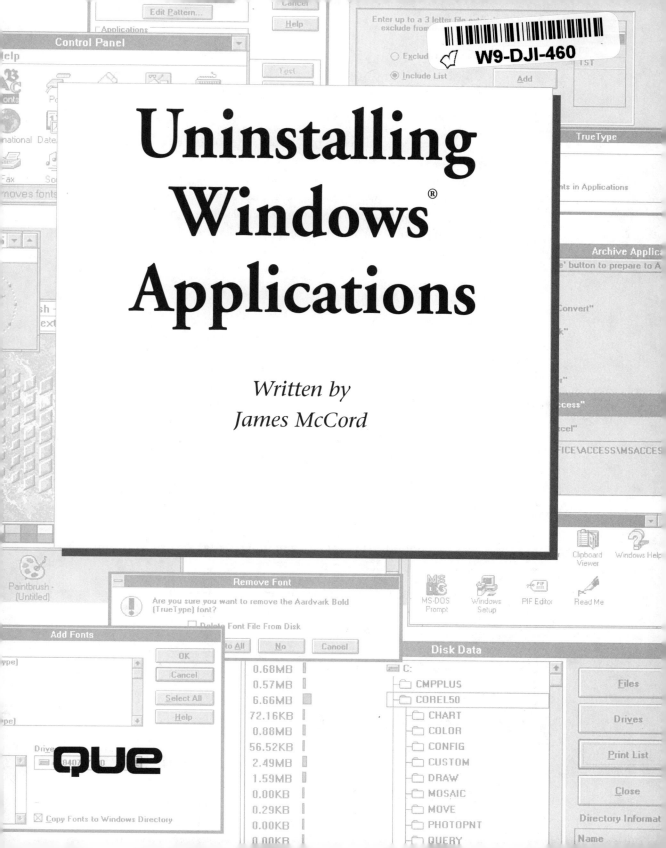

Uninstalling Windows® Applications

Written by
James McCord

que

Uninstalling Windows Applications

Copyright© 1995 by Que® Corporation

Library of Congress Catalog No.: 95-69250

ISBN: 0-7897-0358-0

97 96 95   3 2

Interpretation of the printing code: the rightmost double-digit number is the year of the book's printing; the rightmost single-digit number, the number of the book's printing. For example, a printing code of 95-1 shows that the first printing of the book occurred in 1995.

Screen reproductions in this book were created with Collage Plus from Inner Media, Inc., Hollis, NH.

Publisher: Roland Elgey

Associate Publisher: Joseph B. Wikert

Director of Editorial Services: Elizabeth Keaffaber

Managing Editor: Sandy Doell

Director of Marketing: Lynn E. Zingraf

Credits

Acquisitions Editor
Lori A. Jordan

Product Director
Stephen L. Miller

Production Editor
Caroline D. Roop

Technical Editor
Rick Ladymon

Acquisitions Coordinator
Angela C. Kozlowski

Operations Coordinator
Patricia J. Brooks

Book Designer
Kim Scott

Cover Designer
Dan Armstrong

Production Team
Steve Adams
Maxine Dillingham
Karen Gregor
Aren Howell
Barry Jorden
Daryl Kessler
Bob LaRoche
Elizabeth Lewis
Michael Thomas

Indexer
Kathy Venable

Composed in *Stone* and *MCPdigital* by Que Corporation

Acknowledgments

I would like to thank the staff at MicroHelp for providing information and insight into UnInstaller 3.0. I would especially like to thank MicroHelp's Tim O'Pry and Bill Locke for their help and support.

Trademark Acknowledgments

All terms mentioned in this book that are known to be trademarks or service marks have been appropriately capitalized. Que Corporation cannot attest to the accuracy of this information. Use of a term in this book should not be regarded as affecting the validity of any trademark or service mark.

About the Author

James McCord is a software engineer in Atlanta, Georgia, and specializes in Windows application development. He has written several popular multimedia CD-ROM titles for the Windows and Macintosh evironments. In addition, James has authored and coauthored twelve computer books including Que's *Borland C++ Programmer's Reference* and *Windows 3.11 Programmer's Reference*.

We'd Like to Hear from You!

As part of our continuing effort to produce books of the highest possible quality, Que would like to hear your comments. To stay competitive, we *really* want you, as a computer book reader and user, to let us know what you like or dislike most about this book or other Que products.

You can mail comments, ideas, or suggestions for improving future editions to the address below, or send us a fax at (317) 581-4663. For the on-line inclined, Macmillan Computer Publishing has a forum on CompuServe (type **GO QUEBOOKS** at any prompt) through which our staff and authors are available for questions and comments. The address of our Internet site is **http://www.mcp.com** (World Wide Web).

In addition to exploring our forum, please feel free to contact me personally to discuss your opinions of this book: on CompuServe, I'm at 76103,1334, and on the Internet, I'm **smiller@que.mcp.com**.

Thanks in advance—your comments will help us to continue publishing the best books available on computer topics in today's market.

Stephen L. Miller
Product Development Specialist
Que Corporation
201 W. 103rd Street
Indianapolis, Indiana 46290
USA

Contents at a Glance

Contents

12 Working with Initialization Files   107

13 Uninstalling Microsoft Office: A Sample Uninstall Session   127

14 Learning about UnInstaller 3.0   139

15 Uninstalling Applications with UnInstaller 3.0   147

16 Using Archive Applications   159

Introduction

Would you ever drive your car 100,000 miles without changing the oil, checking your tires, or tuning the engine? Of course not! A car costs a lot of money and needs proper maintenance to perform well. The same is true for your computer—especially when you are running Windows. You need to properly maintain Windows to keep your system running smoothly.

The best maintenance procedures you can perform to keep Windows and your system running smoothly are to remove unnecessary applications and files and to keep Windows configured properly. When you first install Windows, it analyzes your system and configures itself to match your system. Only the files that Windows needs to operate on your system are copied to your hard drive. In effect, Windows is optimized for your system when it is installed.

As time passes, you inevitably add applications and hardware to your system. Each time you add an application or hardware device, you add more files to your system and change the configuration of Windows. These added files eat up space on your hard drive and the configuration changes consume memory Windows needs to operate properly. Over time, these files and configuration changes add up and Windows slowly loses performance.

To keep Windows running at peak performance, you need to perform periodic maintenance. *Uninstalling Windows Applications* provides the information that you need to effectively maintain Windows. This book takes you through the steps to uninstall Windows applications.

Before you start using this book, you should understand what the term *uninstall*, as used in this book, really means. On the surface, uninstalling an application appears to be the act of removing application files from your hard drive. In many ways, this definition is accurate because a large part of uninstalling an application is removing the application files. However, the uninstall process goes way beyond removing application files. The uninstall process includes analyzing your system, organizing your hard drive, configuring Windows drivers, editing initialization files, and so forth. In effect, the uninstall process that you will learn in this book teaches you how to uninstall applications while optimizing Windows and your system.

Who Should Use This Book?

Uninstalling Windows Applications is the perfect choice for anyone who uses Windows at home, at the office, at school, or wherever. This book is useful for anyone who wants to get the most out of Windows while reclaiming hard disk space and other system resources. This book provides the information that you need to remove applications and configure Windows using standard Windows components. It also teaches you how to use MicroHelp's UnInstaller 3.0 to uninstall applications and to clean up your system.

Uninstalling Windows Applications provides you with three general categories of information. To start, this book teaches you how Windows works and why it works the way that it does. This way you can not only perform the steps to remove applications and optimize your system, you can understand why you are performing these steps and what effect these steps have on your system. Next, you will learn the four steps to uninstalling applications. This book teaches you how to use the standard Windows components to effectively remove applications and to configure your system. The standard Windows components, File Manager, Program Manager, and Control Panel, are presented along with ways they can be used to manually remove application files and settings. The remainder of this book teaches you how to use UnInstaller 3.0 and its features to remove Windows applications and to clean up your system.

This book assumes that you know how to use Microsoft Windows. If you know how to use a mouse and work with any Windows application, you know enough to benefit from *Uninstalling Windows Applications*. This book teaches you what you need to know about how Windows works and outlines all the steps that you need to follow to remove applications and to configure Windows.

How This Book Is Organized

This book is designed to take you, step-by-step, through the process of uninstalling Windows applications and configuring Windows using either the standard Windows components or MicroHelp's UnInstaller 3.0. To accomplish this, the book covers the following areas: the Windows environment, the uninstall process, and UnInstaller 3.0 operation.

The Windows Environment

Chapter 1, "The Windows Concept," introduces you to the Windows environment. Many Windows users are familiar with the way that Windows operates but are not familiar with the functional concepts behind Windows. Chapter 2, "Understanding Applications," helps you to understand the advantages and overall design of Windows. It also helps you understand how Windows applications interface with the Windows environment. You can use this knowledge to more effectively uninstall applications. Chapter 3, "The Many Types of Files," explains the many types of files that you will find on your system. Because Windows and Windows applications are collections of various file types, you will need to understand these file types when you are uninstalling applications.

The Uninstall Process

Chapters 4 through 8 are the heart of this book. These chapters introduce you to the four-step uninstall process. You learn about each step in the process and are presented with detailed instructions on how to perform each step using the standard Windows components. In Chapters 9 through 11, you also learn how to use Program Manager, File Manager, and the Control Panel as your tools to uninstall applications and to configure Windows. Chapter 12, "Working with Initialization Files," discusses the SYSTEM.INI and WIN.INI files and how to edit sections and entries in these files. To summarize what you've learned, in Chapter 13, "Uninstalling Microsoft Office: A Sample Uninstall Session," you see how the four-step uninstall process is used to actually remove a Windows application.

Uninstaller 3.0 Operation

Chapter 14, "Learning about UnInstaller 3.0," introduces you to MicroHelp's UnInstaller 3.0 uninstalling utility. In Chapter 15, "Uninstalling Applications with UnInstaller 3.0," you learn how to use UnInstaller to uninstall Windows applications and to clean up your system. The remaining chapters in this book cover each UnInstaller feature in more depth and how to use these features in the four-step uninstall process.

Crash Recovery

Uninstalling Windows applications, if not performed correctly, can cause any number of problems on your system ranging from an inoperable Windows application to a system that won't boot. Appendix A, "Crash Recovery Procedures," takes you through the steps that you'll need to follow if you make a critical mistake when uninstalling an application. The procedures presented in this appendix help you recover your system, Windows, and any application that may have been affected by the uninstall procedure.

Questions about UnInstaller

Appendix B, "Common UnInstaller Questions," is a list of questions about MicroHelp's UnInstaller. These questions are oriented towards UnInstaller's capabilities and how UnInstaller can be used to perform certain tasks.

What about Windows 95?

This book will help you uninstall Windows 3.x applications from Windows 3.1, Windows for Workgroups 3.x, and Windows 95. Appendix C, "Removing Applications from Windows 95," explains how removing Windows applications from Windows 95 differs from removing applications in Windows 3.1.

MicroHelp's UnInstaller 3.0 is also Windows 95-compatible and can be used to remove Windows applications from Windows 95.

Chapter 1

The Windows Concept

Windows was created to make your life easier. It replaces the DOS command line with an easy-to-use interface that allows you to launch applications, exchange data between applications, manipulate files, and much more. Because it is easy to use, many people have misconceptions about Windows.

The Myth: the Windows architecture provides a layer of protection between you and your system. You don't need to worry about managing and configuring your system because Windows and its applications perform these tasks automatically. Windows-compatible hardware and software come with setup routines that automatically configure your system. All you have to do is stick in the setup disk and start the setup program. What could be easier?

The Reality: while Windows is easy-to-use and offers many advantages to its users, Windows is not perfect. Without proper maintenance and care, Windows will slowly lose its performability. Setup routines provided by software and hardware vendors don't always have your system's best interests in mind. Without keeping a check on your system, you will never get the most out of Windows.

This book is designed to help you maintain and configure Windows for your system. Of course, it focuses on how you uninstall applications and clean up your system. You will also find helpful hints for configuring Windows. Let's start by reviewing the Windows environment. By understanding the Windows environment, you will be better able to perform the steps needed to uninstall applications and clean up your system.

In this chapter, you learn

- The advantages of the Windows environment
- The main components of the Windows interface
- The standard parts of the application window
- The main components of the Windows 95 interface

> **Note**
>
> Throughout this book, the term Windows refers collectively to Windows 3.1 and Windows for Workgroups 3.x. The term Windows 95 will be used whenever topics specific to Windows 95 are discussed.

The Windows Advantage

Microsoft Windows is a graphical user interface (GUI) environment for computer systems running DOS. Windows allows you to work with graphical representations of applications and files instead of working at the DOS command-line. Windows and Windows applications offer many advantages over traditional DOS and DOS-based applications. The primary advantages are multitasking, a common user interface, and device independence.

> **Note**
>
> Although Microsoft claims that Windows is an operating system, Windows is really an operating environment. When Windows is started, it takes control of most of the system's operations. However, Windows still relies on DOS for file access. Windows will not run without DOS and, therefore, is not a true operating system. Windows 95, however, does not require DOS and is a true operating system.

Multitasking

Windows allows you to run more than one application at a time. This capability is called *multitasking*. Under DOS, applications can only be run one at a time. To start an application, you have to exit the application that you are running. In Windows, you can open several applications at one time. In fact, you can have several Windows applications and DOS applications running at the same time. Figure 1.1 shows the Windows environment and its multitasking capability.

Multitasking is advantageous in many ways. The most obvious advantage is that you don't have to close one application to start another. However, there are many advantages that aren't so obvious. For example, applications that are running simultaneously can share data in any one of several ways including the Windows Clipboard, Dynamic Data Exchange (DDE), and Object Linking and Embedding (OLE). With DDE, applications can communicate and exchange information behind the scenes, without requiring you to act as the mediator. OLE is another feature that allows an entire object, and its functionality, to be copied to another application or document.

With the Clipboard, you can cut or copy information from an application and paste that information into another application. The process is simple and is supported by almost all Windows applications. With multitasking, the capabilities of your computer are increased significantly.

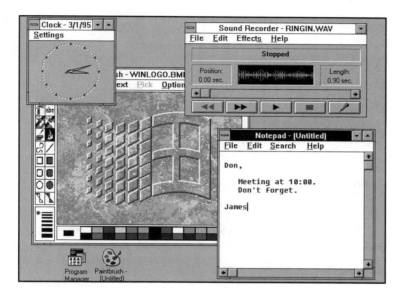

Fig. 1.1
In this figure, several Windows applications are open and running.

Common User Interface

Another strong advantage of Windows is its common user interface. Windows applications look and behave similarly. For example, most Windows applications contain menu bars with common menus such as File, Edit, and Help. Even though two applications perform two separate functions, they look enough alike that you can quickly adjust to new applications. Figures 1.2 and 1.3 show two separate Windows applications. Microsoft Works is shown in word processing mode in Figure 1.2. Notice the menu structure and the overall look of the application. Now look at the Microsoft Money application shown in Figure 1.3. If you compare the figures, you will notice that these applications look somewhat alike even though they perform entirely different functions. The Windows common user interface makes even new applications seem familiar.

Fig. 1.2
The Microsoft
Works application.

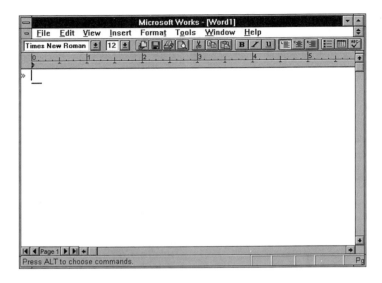

Fig. 1.3
The Microsoft
Money
application.

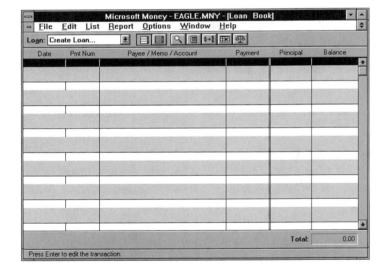

Device Independence

A key feature of Windows that you might not recognize is device independence. With Windows, applications do not talk directly to your system or
its peripherals. Instead, applications talk to Windows in a generic, device-
independent, way. Windows, in turn, passes the generic information to a
device driver. The device driver converts the generic information into
device-dependent information for the hardware peripheral.

Let's look at an example. When you want to print a document from your word processor, you typically choose the Print command from the word processor's File menu. The word processor then passes device-independent information about the file you want to print to Windows. Windows, in turn, passes the information to the printer driver. The printer driver then converts the information into a language that the printer can understand.

On the surface, this may not seem like much of an advantage. However, the advantage is significant to Windows users and software developers. Let's say, for example, you buy a new Hewlett-Packard computer. In the DOS world, this would present a problem for you and software developers: your old software wouldn't support the new printer because the software must provide its own driver for the new printer. Your distribution disks wouldn't contain the printer driver because the printer didn't even exist when the software was created. To support the new printer, each software vendor would have to develop a printer driver that works with the new printer. You couldn't use your old software with your new printer until the software developers created printer drivers for their software. Then, once you actually got the printer driver, you would have to modify each application you use. This obviously is a problem.

In the Windows world, device independence solves this problem. When a new Windows-compatible printer or hardware device is released, it comes with a Windows driver. As a user, you simply need to add the driver to your Windows environment. This one driver works with all Windows applications. The deal gets even sweeter for software developers. Because the hardware manufacturer provides the driver, the software developers don't have to create device drivers for every possible piece of hardware on the market. Everybody wins.

Now that you have seen a few of the major advantages of Windows, let's quickly look at the Windows interface.

The Windows Interface

When you start Windows, the Program Manager window is displayed. *Program Manager* is the main window where you start applications, organize applications, and exit Windows. In fact, Program Manager is your primary tool for managing your applications. The Program Manager window contains a series of program group icons. A *program group* is a set of related applications. By double-clicking a program group icon, the *group window* is displayed. When the group window is opened, you can view the icons that represent the applications in the program group. The icons that represent applications are called *program items*. Double-clicking a program item launches the associated application. Program Manager and all other windows are displayed on the Windows *desktop*. The Windows desktop is the Windows background area. Figure 1.4 shows the desktop, Program Manager, the Main group window, program items in the Main group window, and various program groups.

Fig. 1.4
The Windows
Program Manager.

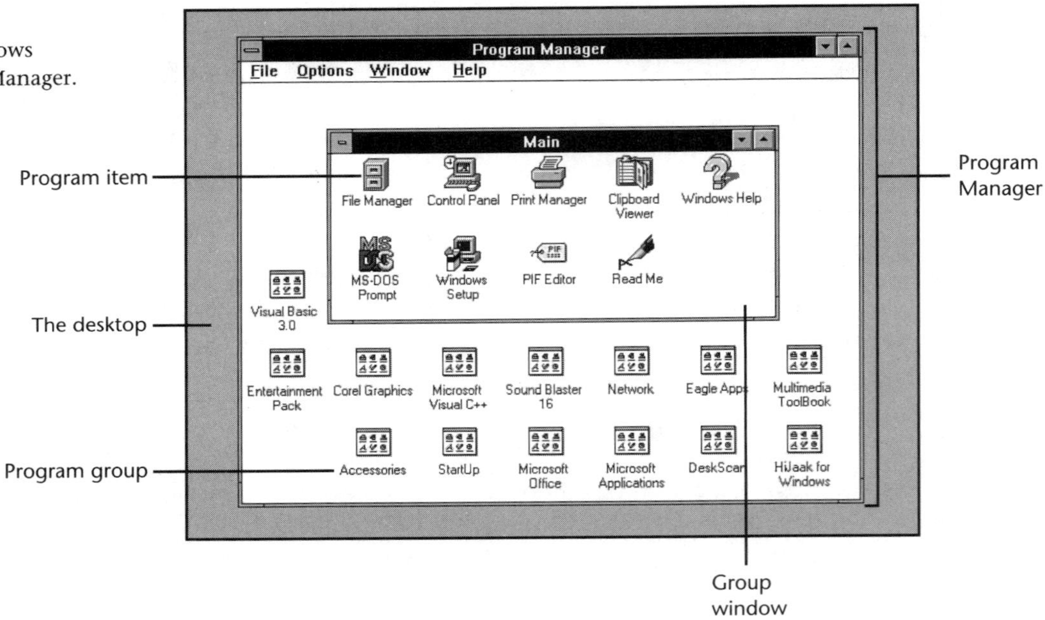

As we just mentioned, Program Manager allows you to start applications. When you start an application, the application is displayed in a window.

The application window is the main window for an application and is the visual interface between you and the application. Most of the application's activity takes place within this window. Figure 1.5 shows an example of an application window and identifies its common components. These components of the application window provide a consistent interface between all Windows applications and make even new applications feel like old friends.

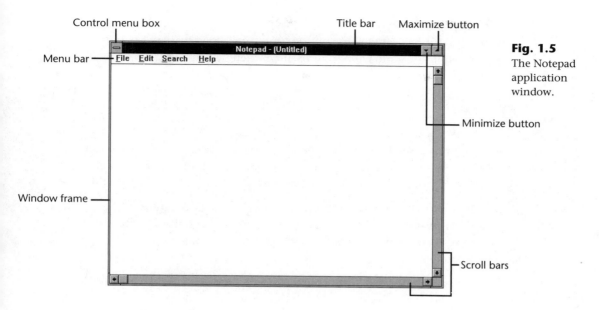

Control menu box   Title bar   Maximize button

Menu bar

Window frame

Fig. 1.5
The Notepad
application
window.

Minimize button

Scroll bars

Exploring the Windows 95 Interface

Windows 95 offers all the advantages of Windows 3.1 and Windows for
Workgroups 3.11 and more. It is a true 32-bit operating system that offers a
new user interface that is more intuitive to novice users and offers more powerful features for advanced users. While Windows 3.1 and Windows for
Workgroups 3.11 users will have some difficulty moving to Windows 95,
these users will find that most of the common Windows 3.1 components
are still there—they just look and act a little differently.

The Windows 95 interface, or desktop, includes the following major
components:

- The Taskbar
- My Computer
- The Network Neighborhood
- The Recycle Bin

The Taskbar

The Taskbar is located at the bottom of the Windows 95 desktop and allows you to quickly launch applications and switch between open applications. The appearance of the Taskbar varies depending on how many applications are open. When no applications are open, the Taskbar only contains the Start button.

The Start button is, in effect, a program launcher. Using the Start button, you can quickly launch programs, open documents, define system settings, access the command-line, and get help. When you click the Start button, a menu appears that contains the following items:

- *Programs*: The Programs menu is used to launch programs and is equivalent to the Windows 3.x Program Manager. This menu contains the equivalent of program groups and program items. Selecting the appropriate program item launches the associated application.

- *Documents*: The Documents menu lists the last 15 documents that were opened in Windows 95. With this menu, you can quickly access the documents that you have been working on most recently.

- *Settings*: The Settings menu allows you to quickly change your system settings and options. With this menu you can quickly access the Control Panel, the Start menu, and the Printers folder.

- *Find*: The Find menu item is a sophisticated search utility. You can search for files using any file criteria including file size, file date, filename, and the date last modified. You can even search for a file using actual text contained in the file.

- *Help*: The Help menu item allows you to quickly access Windows 95 Help.

- *Run*: The Run menu item provides access to the Windows 95 command-line utility.

- *Shutdown*: The Shutdown menu item provides an easy, safe way to log off, restart, or shut down your computer.

When you open an application in Windows 95, a button is added to the Taskbar that contains the name of the application. The Taskbar contains one button for each open application. Using these buttons, you can quickly and easily switch between open applications (this is called task-switching, hence, the name Taskbar).

My Computer

Windows 95 offers My Computer for basic file browsing and file management. You can open a drive by double-clicking the drive icon. Windows 95 then displays the directories (or folders as they are called in Windows 95) on the drive using a drive window. You can then view the contents of a folder by double-clicking the appropriate folder. The contents of the folder are displayed in a separate folder window. You can then review the files and file information.

My Computer's browsing model is very different than what you used with the Windows 3.1 File Manager. The Windows 3.1 File Manager uses a dual-pane window that displays the directory tree on the left and the contents of the selected directory on the right. Microsoft tested the new My Computer browsing model and found that is was easier to use and more intuitive than the dual-pane approach found in the Windows 3.1 File Manager.

If you are used to the Windows 3.1 File Manager for file browsing and file management, Windows 95 provides the Windows 3.1 File Manager for backwards compatibility. In addition, Windows 95 provides the Windows Explorer, which is the Windows 95 dual-pane, file-management utility.

The Network Neighborhood

The Network Neighborhood allows you to browse your network and to gain access to resources not available through My Computer. The Network Neighborhood offers the following:

- *Top-level Configuration*: You can configure the Network Neighborhood to display only the systems, servers, and printers in your workgroup. This feature keeps you from having to view the entire network. Of course, you have the option to view the entire network if you so desire.

- *Support for UNC Pathnames*: Windows 95 supports UNC (Universal Naming Conventions) pathnames making network browsing easy.

- *Network Control Panel*: The Network Control Panel allows you to control the network configuration from a central location. Everything you need for network configuration can be found here.

With the Network Neighborhood, you can quickly and easily perform all the tasks necessary to manage and to configure your network and network connections.

The Recycle Bin

Windows 95 has added a new feature called the Recycle Bin. Any files that are deleted in Windows 95, or in applications that use the Windows 95 common dialog boxes, will be placed in the Recycle Bin.

The files in the Recycle Bin can be placed in a new location, restored to their original location, or removed for permanent deletion. The Recycle Bin provides a layer of protection for you whenever you are removing files. This is especially helpful during the uninstall process because the Recycle Bin allows you to restore deleted files.

From Here...

Now that you have a better understanding of Windows, you are ready to learn the basics of applications in the Windows environment. In the following chapters, you are introduced to the fundamental concepts that you need to know to effectively manage Windows and your Windows applications:

- Chapter 2, "Understanding Applications," teaches you about applications and how they interface with Windows.

- Chapter 3, "The Many Types of Files," introduces the various files and file types that are used by Windows.

Chapter 2

Understanding Applications

Applications are special software programs that allow you to perform tasks on your computer. Common applications include word processors, spreadsheets, databases, and communications. In this chapter, we'll take a brief look at how Windows applications work and how they interface with your system.

In this chapter, you learn

- How Windows operates and handles system events
- Why Windows implements a device-independent architecture

The information presented in this chapter addresses Windows 3.x applications. However, Windows 95 applications are very similar to Windows 3.x applications because they operate using the same principles.

Windows Applications

Windows applications are specifically designed for the Windows environment and all its advantages. Windows-based applications offer a common user interface. For example, Word for Windows and WordPerfect for Windows look and act similarly. Although these applications differ, they use common components to perform the task of word processing. A Word for Windows user can move to WordPerfect for Windows fairly easily, and vice versa, due to the common interface between these applications.

Windows-based applications are also designed to run in a multitasking environment. A Windows application does not have exclusive access to the system. Instead, Windows applications request system resources from Windows.

Windows manages these resources and controls the system. Windows applications also have the capability to share data and communicate with other Windows applications.

Windows and Windows applications are event-driven. This means that you control the way that Windows acts, not the other way around. Windows does nothing until an event happens. Events are typically requests from the user in the form of keyboard or mouse input. Events can also be requests from other applications or system services.

Windows Controls Program Requests

Figure 2.1 shows the way that Windows handles user input or application requests. Windows captures all input to the system. It doesn't matter if the input is from the keyboard, mouse, communications port, or wherever. Windows handles it. Once Windows gets the input, it classifies the input as a certain type of event (mouse event or keystroke) and determines which application is supposed to receive the input. The input is then passed to the appropriate application. The application then processes the input as it sees fit.

Fig. 2.1
User input and Windows applications.

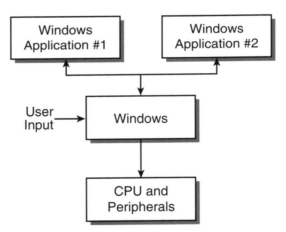

As you can see from Figure 2.1, two types of input can be processed at the same time for two different applications using Windows. For example, you can be typing in your word processor while your communications program is downloading a file. Windows knows which input goes to each application.

Once an application receives input and processes it, the application can request services, such as printing, through Windows. It is important to understand that Windows applications do not directly control the system or system hardware. Windows handles requests from applications using a device-independent layer. Let's take a closer look at the Windows architecture as it applies to device independence.

Application Device Independence under Windows

As discussed in Chapter 1, "The Windows Concept," one of the major advantages of Windows is its device independence. To understand Windows device independence, you need to understand the basic Windows architecture as shown in Figure 2.2.

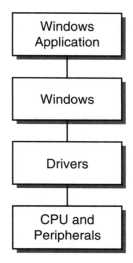

Fig. 2.2
The Windows device-independent architecture.

The top of the Windows architecture is the Windows application. As you can see from Figure 2.2, Windows applications are at the opposite end of the actual computer system. Applications have to go through two architectural layers to get to the system. Whenever a Windows application needs to access hardware to perform a task, such as printing, it has to go through Windows.

Windows has internal, device-independent definitions for manipulating graphical information. Windows applications process information using the Windows device-independent information and ignore the format of output devices. When an application wants to send output to a device, it sends device-independent information to Windows.

Windows Determines the Target Device

Windows understands and accepts the device-independent information passed from Windows applications. Windows then determines the target device that should receive the output and passes the device-independent information to the device driver for the output device. A device driver is a special software file that tells Windows how to communicate with a particular hardware device (printer, display adapter, network card, etc.). The device driver is used to convert the Windows device-independent information into commands that the hardware device can recognize and use.

The Windows device-independent layer is used for both input and output. Windows relies very heavily on device drivers and uses them for each component of the computer system including the keyboard, display adapter, printer, network, sound card, and mouse. As you have seen from the brief overview presented in this chapter, Windows applications are more powerful and flexible than DOS applications. Windows applications take advantage of the power of Windows, including device independence, through the Windows application programming interface (API).

The Windows application programming interface (API) is an extensive set of functions provided with Windows for system services, windows management, graphics manipulation, multimedia control, and more. These functions are an integral part of Windows. Windows applications can call on these functions to perform tasks within the application. For example, when a Windows application starts, it uses API calls to create an application window and to perform its initial screen output. Using API calls assures that Windows applications will work with Windows in a device-independent manner.

From Here...

Now that you are familiar with the differences between DOS and Windows, and understand the structure of Windows and its device-independent layer, you are ready to learn about the different types of files that Windows uses.

- Chapter 3, "The Many Types of Files," introduces the various files and file types that are used by Windows.

- Chapter 4, "Learning the Uninstall Process," explains the basic procedure for removing applications and application files from your system.

Chapter 3

The Many Types of Files

Windows is more than just the graphics you see on the screen. Windows is a complex set of files that allows you to interface with your computer. These files work together to provide all the services that you need, from video display to printer communications.

When you are configuring your system and uninstalling applications, it is important to recognize the different types of files on your system and how many of them work together. By understanding the various types of files and their locations, you can work more effectively during uninstall and cleanup sessions. Windows works with dozens of different types of files. The most common file types are presented in this chapter.

In this chapter, you learn

- The different types of files Windows supports

- The purpose of these different file types

- The typical location of these file types

This chapter presents file types you will find in Windows 3.1 and Windows for Workgroups. Windows 95 supports these file types because Windows 95 is Windows 3.1-compatible.

The File Jungle

Have you ever really examined your hard drive? If you have, you will find thousands of files in dozens of directories. Sorting through the files on your hard drive can be about as difficult and intimidating as walking through a jungle. If you are lucky, you can recognize directories on your hard drive by their name. For example, the C:\DOS directory contains DOS. However, if you look at the contents of any directory on your system, I'll bet you can't identify even one-third of the files in the subdirectory. That's because most of the files in a subdirectory are used by the application and are never directly used by you.

When you uninstall applications and configure your system, you'll need to be able to identify the various types of files and determine how these files are being used. In this chapter, we'll review the most common types of files and where you will find them on your system. We'll look at the following file types presented in alphabetical order:

.CPL files	Help files
DOS support files	.INF files
Driver files	Initialization files
Dynamic Link Library files	.PIF files
Executable files	Virtual device drivers
Font files	Other file types
Group files	

.CPL Files

The Windows Control Panel contains a series of icons that represent applets. The Control Panel applets are utilities you can use to configure your system. Some of the standard Control Panel applets include Fonts, Drivers, Desktop, and Colors. Software and hardware vendors often install applets into the Control Panel so that you can easily configure the software or hardware provided by the vendor. When you double-click an icon in the Control Panel, you launch the corresponding applet. Applet files have the .CPL file extension. The .CPL files are found in the WINDOWS\SYSTEM directory.

DOS Support Files

Windows provides two files to support DOS applications. These are WINOLDAP and the grabber file. WINOLDAP supports data exchange between DOS applications and Windows. Two versions of WINOLDAP are provided for the two Windows operating modes. In standard mode, the file WINOLDAP.MOD is used. In extended mode, the file WINOA386.MOD is used. Windows installs a grabber file that best supports your system. A grabber file with the .2GR extension is installed when you run Windows in standard mode. The actual name of the .2GR file that is copied to your system depends on your system's display capability (VGA, EGA, etc.). The .2GR grabber file enables you to use the Print Screen key to capture the screen and to cut and paste text between DOS and Windows applications.

A grabber file with the .3GR extension is installed when you run Windows in enhanced mode. The actual name of the .3GR file that is copied to your system depends on your system's display capability (VGA, EGA, etc.). The .3GR grabber file supports the Print Screen key for screen capture, copies data from DOS applications, displays DOS data in a virtual window, and copies graphics to the Windows clipboard. Your .2GR or .3GR files can be found in the WINDOWS\SYSTEM directory.

Driver Files

Device drivers allow you to interface hardware with Windows. A device driver is an interpreter between Windows and a hardware device. If you recall from the previous two chapters, Windows and Windows programs workin a device-independent manner. Hardware, on the other hand, is device-dependent. Most hardware has its own proprietary language. The device driver converts the device-independent Windows language into the device-dependent language that the hardware supports.

Windows supports several types of device drivers including drivers for keyboards, display adapters, printers, sound cards, and the mouse. Device drivers (with the exception of virtual device drivers, which are explained later in this chapter), have the .DRV file extension. Device drivers for your keyboard and display adapter are installed automatically when you install Windows. Other drivers can be installed through the Control Panel applets. You can find most of your driver (.DRV) files in your WINDOWS\SYSTEM directory.

Dynamic Link Library Files

Dynamic Link Library files (.DLLs) are the backbone of Windows. The .DLL files are special executable files that can be used by any application. Each .DLL provides routines for performing certain types of tasks. For example, a .DLL may contain spell-checking routines. Another may contain video routines. If you look at your WINDOWS and WINDOWS\SYSTEM directories, you'll see dozens (maybe even hundreds) of .DLL files.

The role of a .DLL file is pretty simple. The .DLL is copied to your hard drive and it simply waits there until it is needed. When a Windows application needs to use one of the routines in the .DLL, the application loads the .DLL and uses the routines. When the application is through with the .DLL, it unloads the .DLL. This process makes efficient use of memory and system resources because the .DLL is only loaded when needed.

Dynamic link library files usually have the .DLL file extension; however, sometimes they have the .EXE file extension. .DLLs can have any valid file extension, though most use the .DLL or .EXE extensions. Most .DLLs are found in the WINDOWS and WINDOWS\SYSTEM directories. Many software applications, however, copy .DLLs into the application directory.

Executable Files

Executable files are typically program files and have the .EXE extension. However, not all .EXE files are program files; some .EXE files are actually .DLLs. Executable files are usually easy to identify because the name of the file usually corresponds to the name of the application. You can find application files in almost every directory on your hard drive. Most applications install their .EXE files in the application directory. Some applications, however, copy their .EXE files to the WINDOWS directory.

Font Files

Windows supports a number of different types of fonts. The three primary types of fonts that Windows supports are raster, vector, and TrueType fonts. Raster font files are also called bitmap font files. Windows uses the raster fonts for screen displays but they can be used for other purposes. Raster fonts are designed for a particular screen resolution and aspect ratio (VGA, EGA, etc.) and use bitmaps to represent characters. For example, raster fonts designed for EGA cards would not look right on VGA cards because EGA and VGA cards have different aspect ratios. Raster font files typically have an .FON file extension and are found in the WINDOWS\SYSTEM directory.

Vector font files describe the characters in the font as a series of lines and curves and are easily scaled to any size. Vector fonts typically have an .FON file extension and are found in the WINDOWS\SYSTEM directory.

TrueType fonts are the most powerful fonts supported by Windows. TrueType fonts are scalable and can be downloaded to most printers and output devices. Each TrueType font requires two files: a .TTF file and an .FOT file. These files are usually found in the WINDOWS\SYSTEM directory.

Group Files

Program groups are used by Program Manager to group your applications. Each program group you find in Program Manager has a corresponding group file. A group file describes the location of the program group in the Program Manager window and contains vital information about each of the program items in the program group. Program item information includes icon position, application command-line, program item description, the application working directory, and the program item icon.

Group files are typically created when you install Windows and Windows applications. You can find your group files in the WINDOWS directory. Group files have the .GRP file extension.

Help Files

Windows supports on-line help through help files. Help files provide useful information about Windows and Windows applications. Most applications install help files. These files are special files that work with the Windows Help application. The information in a help file is formatted in such a way that the Windows Help utility can display useful, navigable information based on the contents of the file using the standard Help format.

Help files have the .HLP file extension. You can find help files all over your system. The most likely location of an application's help file(s) is in the application's directory. You will also find help files in your WINDOWS and WINDOWS\SYSTEM directories.

.INF Files

Windows uses information files to keep track of certain configurations for drivers and installation options. Information, or .INF, files are typically found on the floppy disks used for installation. Several .INF files are typically copied to your WINDOWS and WINDOWS\SYSTEM directories during the installation of Windows. These files are not needed unless you attempt to configure drivers or to install new components.

Initialization Files

When Windows starts, it reads several initialization files. These files tell Windows what to load and how to configure itself. Windows applications also create initialization files that are used by that application to store application-specific information.

Windows uses the Windows initialization files at startup time. The most well-known Windows initialization files are SYSTEM.INI and WIN.INI. Initialization files used by individual applications are called *private* initialization files.

Windows initialization files (found in the WINDOWS directory) and private initialization files (found in either the application's directory or in the WINDOWS directory) have the .INI file extension. When Windows is first loaded, your system should contain about a dozen initialization (.INI) files. Depending on the number of applications that you have on your system, you can have several dozen initialization files.

.PIF Files

.PIF files are used by Windows to control how DOS applications are executed under Windows. Whenever a program item is created in Windows for DOS-based programs, a .PIF file is created. The .PIF file specifies startup parameters, configures video memory and RAM, defines the operating mode, and so on. PIF files can be found in the WINDOWS directory.

Virtual Device Drivers

A virtual device driver is a special type of device driver. Virtual device drivers (VxDs) are 32-bit, protected-mode dynamic link libraries. A VxD manages a particular hardware device or software application. With VxDs, the hardware or software can be used by more than one resource at a time.

When Windows is running in 386 enhanced mode, Windows can take advantage of virtual memory and virtual device drivers. Most virtual device drivers used by Windows have the .386 file extension and can be found in the WINDOWS\SYSTEM directory.

Other File Types

The files presented up to this point in the chapter represent only the most common of the many file types that you will find on your system. The following table shows other file types and extensions that you may run across:

File Type	Common Extensions
Runtime files	.TBK, .VBX, .DLL
Batch files	.BAT
Command files	.COM
Archive files	.ZIP, .ARC
Text files	.DOC, .WPF, .TXT, .WRI, .RTF
Data files	.DAT, .XLS, .123
Backup files	.BAK
Temporary files	.TMP
Graphics files	.BMP, .PCX, .CDR, .TIF, .CGM, .EPS

From Here...

Now that you have learned to identify the most common types of files, you are ready to learn how to uninstall applications and to manage your system.

- Chapter 4, "Learning the Uninstall Process," explains the basic procedures for removing applications and application files from your system.

- Chapter 5, "Step 1: Preparing Your System," teaches you how to get prepared for uninstalling an application.

- Chapter 6, "Step 2: Removing Application Files," teaches you how to remove application files, icons, and settings.

- Chapter 7, "Step 3: Editing Your Initialization Files," teaches you how to review and edit your initialization files.

- Chapter 8, "Step 4: Cleaning Up," teaches you how to complete the uninstall process by removing unwanted files.

Chapter 4

Learning the Uninstall Process

Before we get into the uninstall process, let's quickly review how you'll use this chapter and part of the book. In this chapter, you'll learn the four-step uninstall process. As you learn this process, you will be referred to information found in Chapters 5, 6, 7, and 8. These chapters outline detailed procedures that you can use to perform the various steps in the uninstall process.

The four-step uninstall process involves optional substeps that may be required to uninstall certain types of applications.

Understanding the Four-Step Uninstall Process

When you are uninstalling an application from Windows, you need to perform the following four basic steps:

- Step 1: Preparing Your System

- Step 2: Removing Application Files

- Step 3: Editing Your Initialization Files

- Step 4: Cleaning Up Your System

As you recall, a Windows application is a collection of different types of files. When an application is installed, the application's setup routine copies files to your system in one or more directories. The setup routine may also modify the Windows initialization files, SYSTEM.INI and WIN.INI, and the DOS startup files, AUTOEXEC.BAT and CONFIG.SYS. To completely remove files added by the application and restore all modifications made to initialization and startup files, you need to follow some type of ordered procedure. The four-step uninstall process introduced in this chapter will help you effectively remove as much of an application as safely possible.

> **Note**
>
> This four-step uninstall process is to be used when you are manually uninstalling an application using only the standard Windows components provided with Windows (Program Manager, the Control Panel, and File Manager). If you are using an uninstall utility such as UnInstaller, use the capabilities of the utility to perform these basic steps. Chapter 15, "Uninstalling Applications with UnInstaller 3.0," outlines how the uninstall process is changed when using UnInstaller.

Preparing Your System

The first step in the four-step uninstall process prepares you and your system for the uninstall process. This step is important because it performs the following:

- Gathers the information that you need to make effective uninstall decisions

- Creates backups of important files

- Organizes your files and directories

In this first step, you will need to get as much information about your system as you possibly can. You will be better able to make uninstall decisions if you have good system information. You also need to create backups of your files. You need to, at least, create backups of your system files. Optimally, you should back up your entire system and organize your files and directories and identify those files that can be removed from your system. Chapter 5, "Step 1: Preparing Your System," describes the first step in detail.

Removing Application Files

The second step of the four-step uninstall process involves the actual removal of the application files. In this step, you will do the following:

- Delete the application program items and group

- Delete the application files and directory

- Delete other application files such as fonts and drivers

The second step is the heart of the uninstall process. In this step you will be deleting the majority of the files that will be deleted in the entire process. To effectively perform this step, use the Windows Program Manager and File Manager. Chapter 6, "Step 2: Removing Application Files," explains the second step in detail.

In Windows 95, the Start button's Programs menu replaces Program Manager. Windows 95 provides My Computer, the Windows Explorer, and the Windows 3.1 File Manager for file management.

Editing Your Initialization Files

The third step in the uninstall process is to edit your Windows initialization and DOS startup files. In this step you edit and review the following files: SYSTEM.INI, WIN.INI, AUTOEXEC.BAT, and the CONFIG.SYS.

This third step is very important and very tricky. If you modify or delete the wrong items in these files, your system may crash. If you don't remove references to the application that you are uninstalling, however, you may waste system resources or cause other unpredictable behaviors in Windows. Chapter 7, "Step 3: Editing Your Initialization Files," explains the third step in detail.

Windows 95 and Windows 95 applications use the Windows 95 Registry to store information typically found in initialization files. However, because Windows 95 is Windows 3.1-compatible, it still provides and supports initialization files.

Cleaning Up Your System

The last step of the uninstall process is a general system cleaning process. In this step you will do the following:

- Remove unused and outdated files

- Remove unused Windows components

- Remove temporary files

- Defragment your hard drive

This fourth and final step will help you to clean your system of unwanted files and to reclaim space on your hard drive. Chapter 8, "Step 4: Cleaning Up," explains this step in detail.

In the next four chapters, we will look at each step and substep in the uninstall process. As you review each step and substep, you can decide which of these steps you want to perform.

From Here...

Now that you have reviewed the four basic steps in the uninstall process, you are ready to take a closer look at the first step of the uninstall process—preparing your system.

- Chapter 5, "Step 1: Preparing Your System," teaches you how to get prepared for uninstalling an application.

- Chapter 6, "Step 2: Removing Application Files," teaches you how to remove the application files, icons, and settings.

- Chapter 7, "Step 3: Editing Your Initialization Files," teaches you how to review and edit your initialization files.

- Chapter 8, "Step 4: Cleaning Up," teaches you how to complete the uninstall process by removing unwanted files.

Chapter 5

Step 1: Preparing Your System

The first step in the uninstall process is to prepare your system. In this first step, you will use several tools that will help prepare you and your system for the uninstall process. This step has five substeps as follows:

- Getting system information

- Creating the BOOTLOG.TXT file

- Reviewing the Windows files

- Moving and organizing your files and directories

- Backing up your system

Getting System Information

To effectively uninstall an application, you need to know several types of information about your system and your application. You should know everything you can about your system configuration (display adapter, drives, expansion cards, and so forth) and about the applications on your system (application directory, application settings, drivers used, and so forth). You can get this information in many different ways using the various tools available on your system.

Recording System Information

In order to effectively remove applications and to clean up your system, you need to know about Windows and its relationship with your system and applications. The exact configuration of Windows is different for every computer because the Windows configuration depends on the hardware and software installed on the system. You can get the system information that you need by reviewing your initialization files, your fonts, your file associations, and your drivers.

Reviewing Your Initialization Files

Before you start deleting files, you need to review your Windows initialization files. The Windows initialization files, WIN.INI and SYSTEM.INI, are very important. Go ahead and print a copy of these files so that you can reference them throughout the uninstall process. As you begin to uninstall an application, you will need to look at the many sections in these files to determine what parts need to be modified or deleted. Having a printout handy will save you some time in the uninstall process.

To print a copy of the Windows initialization file, open the WIN.INI and SYSTEM.INI files using your favorite word processor, Write, or Notepad and print the file. The WIN.INI and SYSTEM.INI files can be found in your WINDOWS directory. However, do not edit or save the files at this time. See Chapter 12, "Working with Initialization Files," to better understand the purpose, types, and format of initialization files and for detailed information on the sections and entries in the SYSTEM.INI and WIN.INI files.

Caution

The WIN.INI and SYSTEM.INI files are simple ASCII files. If you open these files using a word processor such as Word or Write, then accidentally save them, you may corrupt the file. To be safe, use Notepad (a simple text editor) to open and print these files.

Because Windows 95 is compatible with Windows 3.1 and Windows 3.1 applications, you will still find initialization files used with Windows 95. Windows 3.1 applications will use initialization files to store configuration information and settings while Windows 95 applications will use the Windows 95 Registry to store configuration information and settings. You can use the Registry Editor to make changes to the Windows 95 Registry.

Reviewing Your Fonts

Windows keeps one list of installed fonts. Any application that installs fonts adds fonts to this list. To view the Windows list of installed fonts, go to the Control Panel and open the Fonts applet.

The Fonts applet displays a list of fonts installed in Windows. At this time, you need to review the list of fonts and determine which fonts you want to keep and which fonts you want to remove. As you are making note of the fonts you want to delete, be aware that some of the fonts that you don't use are actually used by Windows. Do not delete fonts that are standard to Windows.

Windows 95 uses the Fonts folder found in the Control Panel to install and remove fonts from the Windows 95 system.

Reviewing File Associations

Windows uses file associations to link certain types of files with applications. For example, Windows associates all files with the .WRI file extension with the Microsoft Write word processor provided with Windows. File associations are important during the uninstall process so that you can determine which document files (if any) are associated with the application that you are deleting.

To determine whether the application has a file association, review the [extensions] section of the WIN.INI file, which defines the associations for Windows applications and files. The [extensions] section of the WIN.INI file contains entries that associate a three-letter file extension (.DOC, .TXT, .WRI, and so on) with the application's executable file. Table 5.1 lists the Windows standard file extensions.

Tip

As a general rule, don't delete the font files with the .FON extension because these fonts are used by Windows for screen displays.

Tip

If you know the type of document files produced by the application you are deleting, make a note of these files. Therefore you don't have to review the [extensions] section of WIN.INI.

Table 5.1   Standard File Extensions

File Extension	Associated Application	Executable File
.BMP	PaintBrush	PBRUSH.EXE
.CAL	Calendar	CALENDAR.EXE
.CLP	Clipboard Viewer	CLIPBRD.EXE
.CRD	Cardfile	CARDFILE.EXE
.HLP	Windows Help	WINHELP.EXE
.INI	Notepad	NOTEPAD.EXE

(continues)

Table 5.1 Continued		
File Extension	**Associated Application**	**Executable File**
.MID	Media Player	MPLAYER.EXE
.MMM	Media Player	MPLAYER.EXE
.PCX	Paintbrush	PBRUSH.EXE
.REC	Macro Recorder	RECORDER.EXE
.RMI	Media Player	MPLAYER.EXE
.TRM	Terminal	TERMINAL.EXE
.TXT	Notepad	NOTEPAD.EXE
.WAV	Sound Recorder	SOUNDREC.EXE
.WRI	Write	WRITE.EXE

If the application you are removing has a file association, note the file association so you can locate, review, and delete all associated files. For example, if you were going to delete the Write program, you would want to locate, review, and delete all files with the .WRI file extension.

 Windows 95 uses file associations. File associations, however, are stored in the Windows 95 Registry. In addition, Windows 95 uses hidden file extensions. Therefore you will not be able to view the extension of a file using the Windows 95 file browsing utilities My Computer and Windows Explorer.

Reviewing Drivers

Windows uses driver files for every peripheral attached to your system including the display adapter, printer, mouse, and sound card. Review your list of installed drivers at this time. To do this you need to use several Windows tools.

Let's start by looking at the printers installed on your system. You can review your list of installed printers by using the Control Panel Printers applet. Open the Printers applet and make a note of which printers are currently installed. If the list contains a printer that you no longer use, note which printer needs to be removed. For more information on viewing your list of installed printers, see Chapter 11, "Using the Control Panel."

Now that you have made your list of installed printers, review your printout of the WIN.INI file. Look over the [printerPorts] section. This section contains entries that you can use to determine the name of the printer driver associated with each printer installed on your system. Make a note of the name of each printer driver associated with each of your installed printers. Pay particular attention to the names of the drivers associated with the printers that you want to remove. For more information about the WIN.INI file and the [printerPorts] section, see Chapter 12, "Working with Initialization Files."

Now you need to review your list of drivers using the Control Panel Drivers applet. Open the Drivers applet and make a note of which drivers are currently installed on your system. Review the list and determine whether any of the drivers need to be removed.

> **Note**
>
> The Drivers applet deals mainly with multimedia drivers. The display, network, keyboard, and mouse drivers are modified through the Windows Setup routine found in the Main program group. For more information on viewing your list of installed drivers, see Chapter 11, "Using the Control Panel."

Once you have made your list of installed drivers, review the [drivers] section of the SYSTEM.INI file using your printout of the SYSTEM.INI file. This section contains entries you can use to determine the filename associated with each driver. Pay close attention to the filenames of drivers that you want to delete. See Chapter 12, "Working with Initialization Files," for more information about the SYSTEM.INI file and the [drivers] section.

Windows 95's Plug-and-Play functionality is designed to automatically detect hardware connected to your system and to load the appropriate drivers. You really don't need to worry about drivers with Windows 95.

Getting Information from the Program Group and Items

Some of the most important information you need can be obtained easily by reviewing the properties of the program items found in the program group for the application that you want to delete. To get this information, open the program group for the application and select the main program item. See Chapter 9, "Using Program Manager," for information on Program Manager, program groups, and program items.

Once you have selected the main program item, choose File, Properties from the Program Manager menu. Program Manager will then display a dialog box that lists the command line and working directory for the program item. From the command line, you can determine the directory for the application and the name of the application file. For example, a command line of C:\WINWORD\WINWORD.EXE indicates that the application directory is WINWORD on the C drive and the main application file is WINWORD.EXE. The working directory usually indicates where the application places temporary and document files. Make a note of this directory. You now know where to look for application files and document files when you go to delete them later.

> **Note**
>
> Use the Properties dialog box to locate the directory and application file for each program item in the application's program group. Not all application files are found in the application directory. Help files, for example, are often placed in the WINDOWS directory. If you have a Help icon in the program group, you can determine where the application places its help files by reviewing the command line found in the program item's properties listing.

Getting a File List

One of the primary goals when deleting an application is to delete all the files that were installed by that application. What better way to achieve this goal than to determine the actual files that were copied to your system. You can determine the list of possible application files copied to your system by reviewing the directories of your application's setup disks. I say "possible" because the application may not copy all the files on the setup disks to your system. Depending on the choices you make during setup, and the configuration of your system, the application's setup routine may not copy all the files.

Here is an example. Let's say you are removing an application that comes with three disks. To get the list of files that may have been copied to your system, go to File Manager and review the directories of these three disks. Print the directories so you can refer to the file listing later. You can search for the files on the list during Step 2 of the uninstall process described in detail in Chapter 6.

> **Caution**
>
> Many applications install library or driver files that are shared by other applications. Deleting a shared file can cause other applications to crash. Never delete a library (.DLL) or driver (.DRV) file unless you know exactly what it is and which application(s) use it.

Note

When you print a file listing from most setup disks, the file extensions for the files will typically end with an underscore (_) character. The underscore character indicates that the file is compressed. When that file is copied to your system, it is decompressed and the underscore character is replaced with the appropriate character for the file extension.

Windows 95 does not have a Program Manager. Instead, you access applications through the Startup button's Programs menu. Look at the properties sheet for the appropriate application to get the required information.

Creating the BOOTLOG.TXT File

Before you make any significant changes to Windows, create a copy of the BOOTLOG.TXT file. The BOOTLOG.TXT file is a log of startup events generated when Windows is started. To create the BOOTLOG.TXT file, follow these steps:

1. Exit to DOS and type the following at the DOS prompt:

   C:\WIN /B

   During startup, Windows creates a BOOTLOG.TXT (if it doesn't already exist) and stores a log of startup events in the file.

2. After the BOOTLOG.TXT file has been created, rename the file to BOOTLOG1.TXT. To do this, type the following at the DOS prompt:

   RENAME BOOTLOG.TXT BOOTLOG1.TXT

3. Start Windows and make your changes. Exit Windows once you have made all of the necessary changes.

4. Restart Windows from DOS by typing:

   C:\WIN /B

   A new BOOTLOG.TXT file will be created.

If Windows does not start after you have made your modifications, you can compare the old BOOTLOG1.TXT file and new BOOTLOG.TXT file. By comparing these files, you will be able to isolate the problem.

Reviewing the Windows Files

Windows is not a single file. Instead, it is a collection of many different types of files. Deleting one of the files that Windows uses can cause Windows to lose some of its functionality or even make Windows crash. The core Windows system contains the following types of files:

- The WIN.COM file that launches Windows.

- The core .DLLs including kernel files, USER, and GDI. These .DLLs contain code and data for Windows functions.

- The font files for screen displays.

- The driver files for the keyboard, display adapter, system, mouse, printers, networks, multimedia, and other hardware devices.

- The DOS support files for running DOS applications under Windows.

- The initialization files that contain the parameters and configuration settings for Windows.

Windows also uses many files to support the applications provided with Windows. These applications come in the form of accessories, utilities, shells, and games. Table 5.2 lists the applications provided with Windows along with the files associated with each application. Some of the applications described in Table 5.2 are found only in Windows for Workgroups. If you don't use one of these applications, you can remove the files associated with the application. See Chapter 3, "The Many Types of Files," for a more complete description of the types of files that Windows works with.

Table 5.2 Windows Application Files		
Application	**Executable File**	**Associated Files**
Calculator	CALC.EXE	CALC.HLP
Cardfile	CARDFILE.EXE	CARDFILE.HLP
Character Map	CHARMAP.EXE	CHARMAP.HLP
ClipBook Viewer	CLIPBRD.EXE	CLIPBRD.HLP
ClipBook DDE Server	CLIPSRV.EXE	None
Clock	CLOCK.EXE	None

Application	Executable File	Associated Files
Control Panel	CONTROL.EXE	CONTROL.HLP, CONTROL.INI, CPWIN386.CPL, DRIVERS.CPL, LZEXPAND.DLL, MAIN.CPL, MIDIMAP.CPL, SND.CPL, WFWSETUP.DLL, and any other .CPL files found in the WINDOWS\SYSTEM directory.
Dr. Watson	DRWATSON.EXE	None
Media Player	MPLAYER.EXE	MPLAYER.HLP, MMSYSTEM.DLL, and MMTASK.TSK
Microsoft Diagnostics	MSD.EXE	MSD.INI
Hearts Game	MSHEARTS.EXE	MSHEARTS.DLL, CARDS.DLL
MS Mail	MSMAIL.EXE	MSMAIL.HLP, SENDFILE.DLL, AB.DLL, DEMILAYR.DLL, FRAMEWRK.DLL, IMPEXP.DLL, MAILMGR.DLL, MAILSPL.EXE, MAPI.DLL, MSSFS.DLL, STORE.DLL, VFORMS.DLL, and WGPOMGR.DLL
Network DDE Background Application	NETDDE.EXE	NDDEAPI.DLL, NDDENB.DLL
NetWatcher	NETWATCH.EXE	NETWATCH.HLP
Notepad	NOTEPAD.EXE	NOTEPAD.HLP
Object Packager	PACKAGER.EXE	PACKAGER.HLP
Paintbrush	PBRUSH.EXE	PBRUSH.HLP, PBRUSH.DLL
PIF Editor	PIFEDIT.EXE	PIFEDIT.HLP
Print Manager	PRINTMAN.EXE	PRINTMAN.HLP
Program Manager	PROGMAN.EXE	PROGMAN.HLP, PROGMAN.INI
Recorder	RECORDER.EXE	RECORDER.HLP, RECORDER.DLL
Registration Editor	REGEDIT.EXE	REGEDIT.HLP, REGEDITV.HLP, DDEML.DLL, OLECLI.DLL, and OLESVR.DLL.
Schedule+	SCHDPLUS.EXE	SCHDPLUS.HLP, SCHDPLUS.INI, MSREMIND.EXE, SCHEDMSG.DLL, and TRNSCHED.DLL.

Tip

If you see any application in Table 5.2 that you don't use, note the files that you need to remove. You will remove these files later in Chapter 6, "Step 2: Removing Application Files."

(continues)

Table 5.2 Continued		
Application	**Executable File**	**Associated Files**
Shell Library	SHELL.DLL	None
Solitaire game	SOL.EXE	SOL.HLP
SmartDrive	SMARTDRV.EXE	None
Sound Recorder	SOUNDREC.EXE	SOUNDREC.HLP
System Editor	SYSEDIT.EXE	None
Task Manager	TASKMAN.EXE	None
Terminal	TERMINAL.EXE	TERMINAL.HLP
Tool Helper Library	TOOLHELP.DLL	None
Chat	WINCHAT.EXE	WINCHAT.HLP
File Manager	WINFILE.EXE	WINFILE.HLP
Windows Help	WINHELP.EXE	WINHELP.HLP, GLOSSARY.HLP
Performance Meter	WINMETER.EXE	None
Minesweeper game	WINMINE.EXE	WINMINE.HLP
Windows tutorial	WINTUTOR.EXE	WINTUTOR.DAT
Write	WRITE.EXE	WRITE.HLP

The files listed in Table 5.2 do not correspond to the files you will find in Windows 95.

Moving and Organizing Your Files and Directories

This would be a good time to review your directories and files. If you take a look at your directory tree, you will probably find ways that you can arrange your files better. For example, many people create directories for their data files. This is useful in two ways. First, creating data file directories makes it very easy to back up all your data files because they are easy to find and in a central location. Second, when you delete an application directory you do not have to worry about deleting any of your data files. See Chapter 10, "Using File Manager," for information about viewing, moving, creating, renaming, and copying files and directories.

> **Caution**
>
> Before you start reorganizing your files and directories, you need to understand the impact of moving the file or directory. Windows and some applications expect to find files in a certain location. Moving some files and directories can cause errors in Windows. For example, moving a .DLL file out of the WINDOWS directory into a directory that is not defined in the DOS PATH will make that .DLL file unavailable to Windows and Windows applications.

Perhaps the best thing you can do at this point is to review the files and subdirectories in the application directory you want to remove. Copy or move the files and subdirectories you want to keep. As a general rule, you will only need to keep the document files that you created with that application.

Windows 95 provides My Computer for file browsing and file management. In addition to My Computer, Windows 95 includes the Windows Explorer for advanced file management and the Windows 3.1 File Manager for users familiar with Windows 3.1 and Windows for Workgroups.

Backing Up Your System

Before you make any significant changes to your system, such as installing or uninstalling an application, you need to always back up your system. You can perform backups using any of the following methods:

- Back up to floppies using the Backup utility provided with DOS and Windows.

- Copy the files you want to save directly to floppies using File Manager.

- Back up the files to a tape drive.

The backup method that you choose will depend on the amount of data that you need to back up, the hardware that is available to you (tape drive), and the amount of time you have. The Backup utility found in DOS and Windows is good to use with floppies and small amounts of data (20 MB or less). You really need a tape drive to store data larger than 20 MB.

> **Note**
>
> A tape drive is a good investment. Internal tape drives can be purchased for under $200. I suggest you buy an external tape drive that uses the parallel port. These can be purchased for around $250 and are very portable. With a portable tape backup unit, installation is simple and you can even share with your friends or coworkers.

The level of backup you perform depends on the significance of the change that you are making to your system. You can perform backups to any one of the following levels:

- Your initialization files

- Your application directory

- Your WINDOWS directory

- Your entire system

As a minimum, back up your initialization files before every uninstall session. If you want to be able to restore your application after uninstalling it, back up the application directory. If you are going to seriously clean up the WINDOWS directory by deleting files (fonts, drivers, etc.), back up your WINDOWS directory. Ideally, you should back up your entire system. Let's look at each of these backup levels in detail.

 Windows 95 provides the Backup application for backing up files, directories, and drives. It even supports tape drives directly.

Backing Up Your Initialization Files

Before you install or uninstall any application, create a backup copy of your Windows initialization files. Don't skip this step—just do it. Windows uses these files to configure itself for your system. The initialization files will most likely have to be modified whenever you uninstall an application. The changes made to the files can potentially cause problems on your system. If you encounter problems after an uninstall session, the backups of the system files can be used to restore your system by simply copying your backup files to their original locations. Copy the following files to a safe location such as a floppy disk or separate subdirectory on your hard drive (for example C:\BACKUP):

AUTOEXEC.BAT: found in the root directory of your boot drive

CONFIG.SYS: found in the root directory of your boot drive

WIN.INI: found in the WINDOWS directory

SYSTEM.INI: found in the WINDOWS directory

Windows Group (.GRP) files: found in the WINDOWS directory

If you make frequent changes to your Windows environment, you can save a lot of headaches by automatically creating backup versions of all your Windows initialization (.INI) files and group (.GRP) files. Whenever you uninstall an application, the chances are that you will have to make changes to the Windows .INI and .GRP files. By having backups of these files, you can more easily isolate problems such as Windows crashes, applications crashes, missing files, and so forth that can be created by the uninstall process.

You can automatically create backups of the .INI and .GRP files when booting your system by adding the following lines to your AUTOEXEC.BAT file:

```
cd \WINDOWS
copy *.INI *.IBK
copy *.GRP *.GBK
cd \
```

You can use Windows Notepad or SysEdit to edit the AUTOEXEC.BAT file. The AUTOEXEC.BAT file is found in the root directory of your boot drive and is executed when your system is booted. The changes to the AUTOEXEC.BAT file create backup copies of all of your Windows initialization and group files. For example, the WIN.INI file will be copied to WIN.IBK and the MAIN.GRP file will be copied to MAIN.GBK. See Chapter 12, "Working with Initialization Files," for more information on using Notepad and SysEdit.

If you make changes to Windows during the day that cause problems, you can recover the old Windows setup by exiting to DOS and typing the following at the DOS prompt:

```
cd \WINDOWS
copy *.IBK *.INI
copy *.GBK *.GRP
cd \
```

Once the files have been recovered, restart Windows and you'll be back to the Windows setup that you had when you first booted your system.

Backing Up Your Application Directory

Backing up the application directory for the application that you are going to delete is a good idea if you want to restore the application at a later time. When you back up the application directory, keep in mind that Windows applications store files all over the place. Backing up the application directory is no guarantee that you have backed up all of the files used by the application. Therefore, if you want to be able to restore an application, back up the application directory and do not remove any application files found elsewhere on your hard drive.

Tip
If you have the original application setup disks, you may not need to back up your entire application directory. Instead, back up your document files located in the application subdirectory.

Backing Up Your WINDOWS Directory

If you are performing a simple uninstall session, such as removing an application's program group, program items, and directory, you probably don't need to back up your WINDOWS directory. However, if you are going to follow this process completely and remove drivers, fonts, and other components found in the WINDOWS and WINDOWS\SYSTEM directory, you should back up your WINDOWS directory. By backing up your WINDOWS directory, you can restore Windows if you make a mistake.

Caution

As an alternative to backing up the WINDOWS directory, you can use your original Windows setup disks to restore Windows if you make a mistake during the uninstall process. However, many users get Windows preinstalled on their systems without setup disks. If this is how you got Windows, stop everything and make a backup of your WINDOWS directory now! It is better to be safe than sorry.

Backing Up Your Hard Drive

Performing a complete backup of your hard drive is a good practice and should be done before making any major changes to your system. However, this is not practical if you have a large hard drive (100 MB or larger) and no tape drive. If you have a tape drive, or can afford to go buy one, make backups of your system every week and before you install or uninstall applications.

From Here...

Now that you know how to prepare your system for uninstalling an application, you are ready to move to the next step—removing application files.

- Chapter 6, "Step 2: Removing Application Files," teaches you how to remove the application files, icons, and settings.

- Chapter 7, "Step 3: Editing Your Initialization Files," teaches you how to review and edit your initialization files.

- Chapter 8, "Step 4: Cleaning Up," teaches you how to complete the uninstall process by removing unwanted files.

Chapter 6

Step 2: Removing Application Files

In this chapter, we are going to use the information gathered in the previous chapter to delete all the application files that we can find. The following steps are covered in this chapter:

- Deleting program groups and items

- Deleting the application directory

- Removing other application files

The second step of the uninstall process is where you actually delete the application files. If you have followed all the instructions in the previous chapter, "Step 1: Preparing Your System," you will have a stack of information about your system and the application you are deleting. As a minimum, you need to have the following:

- The name of the application directory for the application that you are deleting

- Backup copies of the WIN.INI, SYSTEM.INI, AUTOEXEC.BAT, CONFIG.SYS and Windows Group (.GRP) files on a floppy

- A list of fonts, printers, and drivers that you want to remove from your system.

> **Caution**
>
> The procedures presented in this chapter result in the permanent deletion of files from your system. Use caution before deleting files and make sure that you have read the section in Chapter 5, "Backing Up Your System."

Deleting Program Items and Groups

Almost every Windows application creates its own program group and program items in Program Manager. If the application that you are uninstalling has its own program group, it is easy to remove the program group and all of the application's program items: simply delete the application's program group. When you delete the program group, the program items contained in the group are automatically removed. See Chapter 9, "Using Program Manager," for information on how to delete program groups and program items, respectively.

Removing an application's program items may not always be as simple as removing the application's program group. Some Windows applications, unfortunately, do not create their own program groups. Instead they install their program items into an existing program group such as the Main or Accessories group. You often find this to be the case with utilities or games. You may also have this problem if you have consolidated program items into custom program groups.

To delete the program items for the application when no application program group exists, simply look through all of your program groups and delete any program item that is associated with the application that you are deleting.

> **Note**
>
> Deleting a program group only removes the .GRP file found in the WINDOWS directory. It does not remove that actual application or its files from your hard drive.

 Windows 95 does not have a Program Manager. Instead, Windows 95 uses the Programs Menu that is accessed from the Startup button. You must edit the appropriate property sheet to remove program items from the Windows 95 Programs menu.

Deleting the Application Directory

In Chapter 5, you determined the directory that contained most of the application files. If you can't determine the application directory, you can usually find it by reviewing the directories on your hard drive. The application directory typically has a name that can be associated with the name of the application. For example, Windows uses the WINDOWS directory and Word for Windows uses the WINWORD directory. See Chapter 10, "Using File Manager," for information on viewing and deleting directories.

Once you have located the directory from File Manager, take a few seconds and review the contents of the directory. Make sure that there are no files in the directory that you want to save. If there are files that you want to save, copy or move them before deleting the directory. Once you have reviewed the directory, you can delete it.

Congratulations! You have just performed the major part of the uninstall process. You can quit now, but you really need to finish the process to remove any remaining components of the application and to clean up Windows.

Tip

Before you delete the files in an application directory, make a note of their file dates. If all the files in the application directory have the same file date, you can use the file date to locate stray application files.

Removing Other Application Files

Back in Chapter 5, "Step 1: Preparing Your System," you determined as much information about the application files as you could. This information included files from the setup disks, fonts installed by the application, drivers used by the application, and so forth. In this section, you locate any of the application files that may have been copied to locations other than the application directory. These files are often .DLL, font, drive, help, initialization files, and so forth. During your search for stray application files, you can use the following tricks:

- File dates
- Filenames
- File types
- File properties

Let's look at how you can use each of these methods to locate stray application files.

Using File Dates

You may be asking yourself, "What do I need to know about file dates?" This is a good question with a simple answer. You can often locate stray application files by the date of the file. This is how it works.

Many software vendors distribute application files that all have the same date. This is useful to the software vendor because the date indicates the application version that the file is associated with. Dates provide a simple method of version control. Although not all software vendors distribute application files with the same date, enough do to make it worth checking your directories.

If the application you are deleting used the same file date for all the application files, use File Manager to view your directories sorted by File Date. Use the appropriate file date to locate (and possibly delete) any matching application files.

Using Filenames

Back in Chapter 5, you may have generated a list of application files from the application's setup disk(s). If you did, look through the list for files that are typically copied to the WINDOWS or WINDOWS/SYSTEM directories. These files often have the .DLL, .EXE, .DRV, .INI, or .CPL file extensions. Remember that your list may contain compressed filenames with the .DL_, .EX_, .DR_, .IN_, or .CP_ file extensions. See Chapter 3, "The Many Types of Files," for a description of these file types.

Once you have located any suspect files, you can use the File Manager's Search feature to determine whether the files are on your system.

Using File Types

As you are trying to find stray application files, you often need to locate a particular type of file. This is especially true when you are attempting to delete all the compatible document files on your system. In Step 1 of the uninstall process, you determined the type of document file(s) generated by the application that you are uninstalling.

Once you have determined the file type, you can search through your directories using File Manager and the Sort by Type option. This way you can easily locate files by their file extensions. For example, you can find all the .WRI files associated with the Write application using this option because the files in a directory are grouped by the file extension.

Windows 95 provides My Computer for file browsing and file management. In addition to My Computer, Windows 95 includes the Windows Explorer for advanced file management and the Windows 3.1 File Manager for users familiar with Windows 3.1 and Windows for Workgroups.

Using File Properties

File properties come in handy when you locate a file that you think may be associated with an application. To view the file information for a particular file, highlight the file from within File Manager and choose File, Properties. If you are using Windows for Workgroups 3.11, File Manager displays the version information for the file, if any is provided. The version information includes the vendor name, product name, and a brief description of the file. You can use this information to determine the application that uses the file.

> **Caution**
>
> As a general rule, don't delete any file that has Microsoft listed as vendor and can possibly be shared by more than one application. This is especially true with Microsoft's .DLL files, which are used by Microsoft and third-party applications.

From Here...

Now that you have removed the application files from your system, you are ready to review and edit your initialization files.

- Chapter 7, "Step 3: Editing Your Initialization Files," teaches you how to review and edit your initialization files.

- Chapter 8, "Step 4: Cleaning Up," teaches you how to complete the uninstall process by removing unwanted files.

Step 3: Editing Your Initialization Files

Now that you have deleted the application files, you are ready to review and edit your initialization files. Before you begin, review the basics of initialization files provided in Chapter 12, "Working with Initialization Files." This third step contains the following substeps:

- Reviewing and modifying SYSTEM.INI

- Reviewing and modifying WIN.INI

- Reviewing CONFIG.SYS

- Reviewing AUTOEXEC.BAT

Caution

Always be careful when editing your WIN.INI and SYSTEM.INI initialization files. Deleting an entry or section in WIN.INI or SECTION.INI can cause a number of problems ranging from poor Windows performance to a complete Windows crash. Before editing your initialization files, always make sure that you have a backup of these files. See the section, "Backing Up Your System," in Chapter 5 for more information about backing up your initialization files.

Windows 95 applications do not use initialization files. Instead, Windows 95 applications use the Windows 95 Registry to store configuration information. Use the Registry Editor to edit the Registry for Windows 95 applications that you want to remove.

Although Windows 95 provides the Registry for Windows 95 applications, Windows 95 also supports initialization files for backwards compatibility with Windows 3.1 applications. If you are removing a Windows 3.1 application from Windows 95, you need to edit the initialization files as outlined in this chapter.

Reviewing and Modifying SYSTEM.INI

Applications sometimes create private sections in the SYSTEM.INI file. Look at each section head in the SYSTEM.INI file to determine whether that section pertains to the application files you just deleted. Most of the time, the section head added by an application contains the application name. For example, a section head of [Word] was added by Microsoft Word. If you locate a section added by the application you want to delete, remove the entire section.

You also need to review all sections in the SYSTEM.INI file for any reference to the application or any of its files. The following sections are commonly found in the SYSTEM.INI file:

- The [386Enh] section contains information used by Windows when running in 386 enhanced mode. You do not want to modify most of the entries in this section; however, you may find a device= entry that references a file that was located in your application directory. If you find an entry that has a path to the deleted application directory, remove it. Do not, however, modify any other entries in this section including the following:

A20EnableCount=	keyboard=
BkGndNotifyAtPFault=	KybdPasswd=
device=	local=
display=	LPTnAutoAssign=
EBIOS=	LRULowRateMult=
EISADMA=	LRURateChngTime=
HardDiskDMABuffer=	LRUSweepFreq=
IdleVMWaveUpTime=	LRUSweepLen=
IgnoreInstalledEMM=	LRUSweepLowWater=
InDOSPolling=	LRUSweepReset=

MapPhysAddress=   SysVMEMSLimit=

MaxBPs=   SysVMEMSLocked=

MaxDMAPAddress=   SysVMEMSRequired=

MinUnlockMem=   SysVMV96Locked=

mouse=   SysVMXMSLimit=

network=   SysVMXMSRequired=

NMIReboot=   TimerCriticalSection=

NoWaitNetIO=   TranslateScans=

OverlappedIO=   TrapTimerPorts=

PageOverCommit=   UniqueDOSPSP=

PerformBackfill=   UseInstFile=

PSPIncrement=   VideoBackgroundMsg=

ReserveVideoROM=   VideoSuspendDisable=

ROMScanThreshold=   WindowUpdateTime=

ScrollFrequency=   WOAFont=

SGrabLPT=   XlatBufferSize=

SyncTime=   XMSUMBInitCalls=

SystemROMBreakPoint=

■ The [boot] section specifies various drivers and Windows modules, and you should not have to modify any of this section, in particular, never modify the following entries:

286grabber=   keyboard.drv=

386grabber=   language.dll=

CachedFileHandles=   mouse.drv=

display.drv=   network.drv=

drivers=   system.drv=

■ The [boot.description] section specifies the names of devices that are modified by Windows setup. Do not edit any entries in this section.

- The [drivers] section specifies the names of multimedia devices and is used by the Drivers applet. Do not edit any of this section.

- The [keyboard] section contains information that is necessary for your keyboard to work properly. Do not edit any of this section.

- The [mci] section specifies Media Control Interface (MCI) drivers. Do not edit any of this section.

- The [NonWindowsApp] section contains information used by DOS applications. There is no need to edit any of this information.

- The [standard] section contains information used by Windows when running in standard mode.

Reviewing and Modifying WIN.INI

Applications sometimes create private sections in the WIN.INI file. Review WIN.INI and look at each section head to determine whether that section pertains to the application files you deleted in the previous chapter.

Most of the time, the section head added by an application contains the application name. For example, a section head of [Word] was added by Microsoft Word. If you locate a section added by the application that you just deleted, remove the entire section.

You also need to review all sections in the WIN.INI file for any reference to the application or any of its files. The following sections are commonly found in the WIN.INI file:

- The [colors] section specifies the colors used for the Windows display. Do not modify this section.

- The [desktop] section contains information that Windows uses to control the appearance and positioning of icons and windows. Do not modify this section.

- The [devices] section lists the active output devices that provide backwards compatibility with Windows applications designed for earlier versions of Windows. Do not modify this section.

- The [embedding] section defines the server objects used in object linking and embedding (OLE). The [embedding] section of your WIN.INI file can get quite lengthy. Review this section and remove the line(s) that contain references to the application deleted in the previous chapter.

- The [extensions] section specifies the file extensions that are to be associated with particular applications. Review this section and delete any line(s) that reference the deleted application.

- The [fonts] section lists the font files used by Windows. This section contains useful information that you can use to associate filenames with fonts. However, you should not modify this section directly. Instead, use the Fonts applet to add or remove fonts. The Fonts applet makes the appropriate changes in this section automatically.

- The [fontSubstitutes] section lists font pairs that Windows treats as interchangeable. Do not modify this section.

- The [intl] section describes how items for international countries are displayed. Do not modify this section.

- The [mci extensions] section specifies the file extensions that are to be associated with the Media Control Interface (MCI) devices. Do not modify this section.

- The [network] section describes network connections and settings. Do not modify this section.

- The [ports] section lists the available ports. Do not modify this section.

- The [printerPorts] section lists the active and inactive output devices that can be accessed by Windows. This section provides useful information that you can use to associate printers with driver filenames. Do not modify this section. This section is used by the Printers applet.

- The [programs] section lists any additional paths that Windows will search when attempting to find the application associated with a data file. Delete any reference to the directory of the application that you just deleted.

- The [sound] section lists the sound files associated with each system event. Do not modify this section. This section is used by the Sounds applet.

- The [TrueType] section describes options for using TrueType fonts. Do not modify this section.

- The [Windows] section describes various visual aspects of the Windows environment. Do not modify this section.

- The [Windows Help] section defines various settings used for the Windows Help window and dialog boxes. Do not modify this section.

See Chapter 12, "Working with Initialization Files," for more information about the sections and entries in the WIN.INI file.

Reviewing CONFIG.SYS

The CONFIG.SYS file is loaded by DOS when your system is booted. The CONFIG.SYS file contains entries that load drivers and configure memory before Windows is ever loaded. For the most part, you do not have to modify CONFIG.SYS when you are uninstalling a Windows application.

Reviewing AUTOEXEC.BAT

The AUTOEXEC.BAT file is automatically executed when your system is started. The AUTOEXEC.BAT file contains entries that customize DOS and load drivers, TSRs, and applications. In general, the only part of the AUTOEXEC.BAT file that you may have to modify when deleting a Windows application is the PATH statement. Although most Windows applications don't add their path to the PATH statement, some do. If the directory of the application that you just deleted is referenced in the PATH statement, remove that part of the statement.

> **Note**
>
> Whenever you suspect a problem with a line in the AUTOEXEC.BAT and CONFIG.SYS files, you can use the REM statement to debug the file. The REM, or remark statement, can be placed before any entry in the AUTOEXEC.BAT and CONFIG.SYS files. Simply open the appropriate file with Windows Notepad or DOS Edit and type **REM** before any suspect entry, followed by a space. During bootup, DOS will skip any line that starts with REM. If the problem goes away, you know that the line containing the REM statement is causing the problem.

From Here...

Now that you have reviewed and edited your initialization files, it is time to clean up your system by removing unnecessary and unwanted files from your hard drive.

■ Chapter 8, "Step 4: Cleaning Up," teaches you how to complete the uninstall process by removing unwanted files.

Chapter 8

Step 4: Cleaning Up

Now you're in the home stretch. The fourth and final step of the uninstall process is to clean up your system. You may want to quit now, but invest a few more minutes to complete the cleanup process. In this chapter you are going to perform the following system cleanup steps:

- Removing unused, unnecessary, and outdated files

- Removing unwanted Windows components with Setup

- Removing temporary files

- Defragging your hard drive

Caution

This chapter involves procedures that result in the permanent deletion of files from your system. You should always use extreme caution when deleting files. Before you use the procedures outlined in this chapter, you should have a backup of your system. Review the section, "Backing Up Your System," in Chapter 5 for more information about creating backups.

Removing Unused, Unnecessary, and Outdated Files

During system cleanup, you want to remove as many useless files as possible. In the following sections, we are going to review several ways that you can remove the most common types of useless files that collect on your system over time.

Private Initialization Files

Almost every Windows application places a private initialization file in your WINDOWS directory. If you look at your WINDOWS directory, you will probably find dozens of .INI files. As you remove applications from your system, you may sometimes forget to remove the .INI file associated with that application.

Now is the time to remove the unused .INI files from your system. Using File Manager, go to your WINDOWS directory and view your files by type. Find the .INI files and look at the filenames. The filename of .INI files usually corresponds to the name of the application that uses the .INI file. For example, CLOCK.INI is used by the Windows Clock application. Delete any unused or extraneous .INI files. See Chapter 6, "Step 2: Removing Application Files," for more information on viewing and deleting files.

Drivers and Driver Files

Back in Chapter 5, "Step 1: Preparing Your System," you reviewed your list of drivers using the Control Panel Drivers applet. Now go to the Drivers applet and remove any drivers that you indicated to be removed in Step 1. If you didn't need to remove any drivers, proceed to the next section.

> **Note**
>
> When you use the Drivers applet to remove a driver, you are not removing the driver file from your hard drive. You are removing that driver from the Windows list of available drivers.

Now that you have removed the drivers from the Windows list of available drivers, you need to remove the driver files from your hard drive. Exit the Drivers applet and go to File Manager. In Chapter 5, you determined the driver files that were associated with the drivers you just removed from Windows. Locate these files and delete them. The [drivers] section of your SYSTEM.INI file printout from Step 1 can be used to determine the names of the driver files that you need to delete. See Chapter 11, "Using the Control Panel," for more information about removing drivers from Windows.

 Windows 95 automatically installs and configures the drivers that it needs using Plug-and-Play technologies. Do not add or remove drivers in Windows 95.

Printers and Printer Driver Files

In Chapter 5 you reviewed your list of installed printers and determined whether you should remove any of your printer drivers. If you don't need to remove any printer drivers, proceed to the next section.

Using your list of printers to remove from Windows, go to the Control Panel Printers applet and remove the appropriate printers from the Installed Printers list box.

Note

When you use the Printers applet to remove a printer driver, you are not removing the printer driver file from your hard drive. You are removing that printer driver from the Windows list of installed printers.

Now that you have removed the printer drivers from the Installed Printers list box, you need to remove the printer driver files from your hard drive. Exit the Printers applet and go to File Manager. In Chapter 5, "Step 1: Preparing Your System," you determined the printer driver files that were associated with the printer drivers you just removed from Windows. Locate these files and delete them. The [printerPorts] section of your WIN.INI file printout can be used to determine the names of the printer driver files that you need to delete. See Chapter 11, "Using the Control Panel," for information on removing printers from Windows.

Windows 95 automatically recognizes the printers connected to your system, then loads and configures the appropriate printer drivers. To add or remove printers from Windows 95, use the Printers folder.

Fonts and Font Files

When preparing your system in Step 1, you determined whether you should remove any of your fonts. If you don't need to remove any of your fonts, proceed to the next section.

Using your list of fonts to remove from Windows, go to the Control Panel Fonts applet and remove the appropriate fonts from your Windows list of installed fonts.

Note

When you use the Fonts applet to remove a font, you may optionally remove the associated font file from your hard drive. Click the Remove Font File From Disk check box in the Remove Font dialog box to delete the font file.

For information about removing fonts from Windows, see Chapter 11, "Using the Control Panel."

 Use the Fonts folder to add and remove fonts in Windows 95.

Removing Old Document Files

Document files come in all different types depending on the application that produced the file. Common document types include .BMP, .DOC, .TXT, .WRI, .DAT, .XCL, .123, .WPF, .CDR, .CGM, .WAV, .MID, .AVI, and dozens more. Old document files build up fast because almost every application that you use generates some type of document file. At this time, review your directories and delete any document files you don't need. Believe me, if you do this, you will be amazed at the amount of stuff that you can remove using your computer.

.DLL Files

Dynamic link library (.DLL) files are special files that can be used by any Windows application. .DLL files are added to your WINDOWS and WINDOWS\SYSTEM directories by applications and by Windows. Review the .DLL files on your system and remove any that you know are not being used. For more information on .DLLs and other special files, refer to Chapter 3, "The Many Types of Files."

Caution

Be careful when deleting .DLL files. Deleting a .DLL can cause one or more applications—and even Windows—to crash. You should never delete a .DLL file unless you know exactly what it is used for and which application(s) use it. As a general rule for .DLLs, when in doubt, don't delete them.

Duplicate Files

When Windows is installed it loads many files that are already present on your system because DOS and Windows use many of the same files. Take this time to locate duplicate files. Unfortunately, there is no easy way to do this without a special utility. The only method supported by Windows is to use the Search feature found in File Manager.

If you know the name of the file, you can use the Search feature to determine how many copies of the file are on the drive and where these copies are located. A few of the likely duplicate files that you will find include:

- HIMEM.SYS

- SMARTDRV.EXE

- MSD.EXE

- EMM386.EXE

- RAMDRIVE.SYS

- Various PIF, HLP, and TTF/FOT files

See Chapter 10, "Using File Manager," for information on using the File Manager Search feature.

Windows 95 includes a powerful search utility called Find. The Find utility can be accessed using the Start button. With the Find utility, you can search for files using any file criteria including file size, file date, filename, and the date last modified. You can even search for a file using actual text contained in the file.

Removing Unwanted Windows Components with Setup

Windows allows you to easily remove any unwanted Windows components using the Windows Setup routine found in the Main program group. With the Windows Setup routine, you can remove standard Windows components including accessories and utilities such as Cardfile and Solitaire. To remove unwanted Windows components, choose Options, Add/Remove Components from the Windows Setup menu bar.

Removing Temporary Files

Now it's time to exit Windows so that you can complete the uninstall process. Exit Windows and get to the C:\ prompt so that you can delete any temporary files on your system. You must exit Windows before you start to remove your temporary files.

> **Caution**
>
> Do not delete temporary files when Windows is running because doing so will crash Windows. Exit Windows first.

When Windows runs, it uses temporary files to store information and temporary data. If an application crashes or misbehaves, Windows may not always be able to delete the temporary files that it was using with that application. Furthermore, when Windows locks up or crashes (usually taking your data with it), it leaves behind temporary files that it did not have a chance to delete.

To delete the temporary files on your system, you need to go to your WINDOWS directory and delete the .TMP files that you find there. You also need to go to your TEMP directory and delete any files that you find there. The TEMP directory is defined in your AUTOEXEC.BAT file by the SET TEMP command.

Tip
Always exit Windows before you turn your computer off. This gives Windows a chance to release any files that were being used and reduces the number of temporary files that you will find on your system.

Defragging Your Hard Drive

As you install and uninstall applications, your hard drive can get in pretty bad shape. To get your hard drive back into shape, you need to defragment your disk. Here's why.

DOS uses a simple method to copy files to your hard drive: data is simply copied to the first available space on your hard drive. If the first available space isn't large enough to hold the data, the file is split up, or fragmented. Each available space on the hard drive is filled until all the data has been copied to your hard drive.

Over time, as you copy and delete files from your hard drive, your data will become very fragmented. It takes DOS longer to read data from a fragmented file because it has to look at several different locations on the hard drive to gather the data for the file. MS-DOS Version 6.0 and later include a utility that helps *defragment* your hard drive. Defragment refers to the process of piecing your files together into a contiguous block of file space. This way, DOS doesn't have to gather information from all over your hard drive to load a single file.

It is always a good idea to defragment your hard drive before installing software to ensure that your new files will not be spread out in dozens of locations on your hard drive. You should also defragment your drive after you remove a significant number of files—for example when you uninstall an application. Defragging will improve the performance of your system.

Third-party applications, such as Norton Utilities and PC Tools, can also be used to defragment your hard drive.

Windows 95 includes the Disk Defragmenter application to defragment your hard drive.

Testing Your System

Now it's time to test your system. Reboot and start Windows. If you get any error messages during bootup or Windows startup, you can identify the cause by looking at the error message and reviewing AUTOEXEC.BAT and CONFIG.SYS (if the error occurred during bootup) or WIN.INI and SYSTEM.INI (if the error occurred while starting Windows).

If Windows starts, test your applications to see if they operate correctly. If you have a problem with an application because you accidentally removed a file the application needs, you can usually resolve the problem by reinstalling the application using the original installation disks. If you have a problem with Windows, you can use Windows Setup to reinstall and/or reconfigure Windows. See Appendix A, "Crash Recovery Procedures," if you have a problem getting your system to boot or you cannot get Windows to start.

From Here...

Congratulations! You've just completed the uninstall process. If this is your first time, you probably learned a lot and you'll get better each time you do it. Now that you are familiar with the uninstall process, you are ready to learn more about the Windows configuration tools.

- Chapter 9, "Using Program Manager," explains how you manage your applications.

- Chapter 10, "Using File Manager," explains how you manage your files.

- Chapter 11, "Using the Control Panel," teaches you how to remove drivers and fonts.

- Chapter 12, "Working with Initialization Files," explains how you edit and manage your initialization files.

Chapter 9

Using Program Manager

The Windows Program Manager is your primary tool for managing your programs and is the primary link between you, Windows, and your applications. This chapter introduces you to Program Manager and provides detailed information on how you can use Program Manager for effective application management.

In this chapter, you learn to

- Use Program Manager to manage your applications

- Delete program groups and program items

- Organize and move program items

- Review and edit PROGMAN.INI

This chapter explains how to use the Windows 3.1 and Windows for Workgroups Program Manager. Windows 95 uses the Start button's Programs menu to accomplish the same tasks performed by the Windows Program Manager. Refer to your Windows 95 documentation for information about editing the Programs menu when you delete applications in Windows 95.

Reviewing Program Manager

As discussed in Chapter 1, "The Windows Concept," Program Manager is the main window that you see when Windows starts. From Program Manager, you can start applications, organize applications, and exit Windows. The Program Manager window contains a series of program group icons. A program group is a set of related applications. By double-clicking a program group icon, the group window is displayed. When the group window is opened, you can view the icons that represent the applications in the program group. The icons that represent applications are called program items.

Double-clicking a program item launches the associated application. Figure 9.1 shows Program Manager: the Main group window, program items in the Main group window, and various program groups.

Fig. 9.1
The Windows
Program Manager.

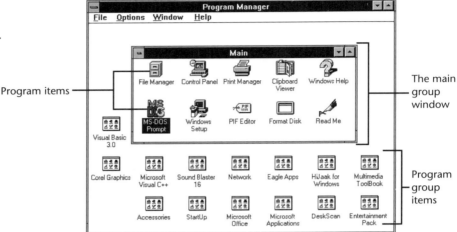

Program items

The main group window

Program group items

Managing Your Applications with Program Manager

Program Manager is an application management tool, which provides two ways to organize your applications: through program groups and program items. Before getting into the details of program groups and program items, you need to first understand how you can use Program Manager and its program groups and program items to effectively manage your applications.

When you run Windows, Windows loads Program Manager (assuming that you are not using a third-party shell such as Dashboard or Norton Desktop). As Program Manager is loaded, Windows reads a series of files from the WINDOWS directory called group files (.GRP). Each group file describes one program group. The group file contains information about the position and name of the program group along with data about each program item in the program group. As Windows reads the group files, it creates the appropriate program groups and items.

As Windows runs, it keeps track of all of the information provided by the group files. Therefore, the more program groups and items you have, the more data Windows has to track. Minimizing the number of program groups and items helps improve Windows performance.

Program Manager plays an important role in two phases of application management: uninstalling applications and cleaning up your system.

Uninstalling Applications with Program Manager

Program Manager plays an important part of the overall uninstall process. Most applications are represented by both program groups and program items in Program Manager. Therefore, you must remove these when uninstalling applications. The processes for removing program groups and program items are described later in this chapter.

You may think that removing an application from Windows is as easy as removing the program group and/or program item from Program Manager. This is not the case. Removing a program item from a program group simply removes the reference to the application from the program group. In other words, the group (.GRP) file for the program group is modified. Removing a program group from Program Manager simply deletes the group (.GRP) file associated with the program group. All the application files remain untouched.

Once the program group and/or program items are removed, you still have several steps to complete before the application is completely removed from your system. See Chapter 4, "Learning the Uninstall Process," for more information on the complete uninstall process.

Cleaning Up Your Program Groups and Program Items

Over time, Program Manager can get pretty cluttered with program groups and program items. Fortunately, Program Manager allows you to clean up by deleting unnecessary program groups and items.

To clean up Program Manager, perform the following maintenance steps:

1. Review your program groups and program items. Delete those that you do not or will not use.

2. Review the remaining program groups and determine whether any of these program groups can be combined. You will often find that Windows applications will create an entire program group for one or two program items. When you find a group with only a few program items, consider combining program groups.

3. Organize your applications. Remember that Program Manager is *your* interface to *your* Windows applications. You can organize your applications in any way you want. The most common way is to organize your

program groups by application category. For example, you can create a program group called Fun and Games and move all of your entertainment program items to it. You can then create another program group called Business Apps for all of your business applications.

Now that you understand Program Manager's role in application management, let's take a closer look at the processes you can use to create, modify, and delete program groups and items.

Deleting Program Groups

When you are uninstalling applications and cleaning up your system, you will usually need to delete one or more program groups. To delete a program group, follow these simple steps:

1. Choose the program group you want to delete by selecting a group icon or a program window. (Windows will delete the current program icon or currently opened program window.) A group icon is selected when the description text is highlighted. The program window is selected when its title bar is highlighted.

2. Choose File, Delete from the Program Manager menu bar, or just press the Del key.

3. The program group and all associated program items will be removed from Program Manager. The group (.GRP) file is also removed from the WINDOWS directory.

> **Note**
>
> Removing a program group from Program Manager only removes the associated group (.GRP) file from the WINDOWS directory. The application files associated with the program group are not removed.

Deleting Program Items

When you are performing a cleanup of your system, or uninstalling an application, you will likely need to remove program items. Program items are easy to delete, simply follow these steps:

1. Select the program item you want to delete. An item is selected when the description text is highlighted.

2. Choose File, Delete from the Program Manager menu bar, or just press the Del key.

3. The program item will be removed from the program group.

> **Note**
>
> Removing a program item from a program group only results in the updating of the group (.GRP) file associated with the program group that contains the program item. The application files associated with the program item are not removed.

Moving Program Items

During system cleanup, you may want to consolidate some of your program items into different program groups. Program Manager allows you to easily move program items between program groups. The following steps are used to move program items with your mouse:

1. Open the program window that contains the program item that you want to move by double-clicking the appropriate group icon. Make sure that the open program window does not cover the group icon for the destination program group.

2. Select the program item you want to move by clicking the item. Hold the mouse button down. Drag the program item to the group icon for the destination program group and release the mouse button. The program item will be moved to the destination program group.

3. Once the program item has been copied, you may need to rearrange the program items in the destination and source program groups. You can do this by opening the appropriate program group and moving the program items around the program window. Then choose Window, Arrange Icons from the Program Manager menu bar. This will space the icons evenly in the program window.

Understanding PROGMAN.INI

As with most Windows applications, Program Manager has an initialization file associated with it—PROGMAN.INI. PROGMAN.INI usually has two sections, [settings] and [groups], that control the position and appearance of items displayed in Program Manager. A [restrictions] section can be added to limit the types of modifications that can be made to Program Manager. You can use the entries in PROGMAN.INI to customize Program Manager before and after an application has been uninstalled.

The [settings] section of PROGMAN.INI typically has five entries. Table 9.1 lists and describes each of these.

Table 9.1 The PROGMAN.INI [settings] Section	
Entry	**Description**
Window=	Indicates the position of the upper-left and lower-right coordinates of the Program Manager window. The last number indicates the state of the Program Manager window (maximized, restored, or minimized).
SaveSettings=	Indicates whether the Save Settings on Exit option of the Program Manager Options menu is selected. This value is 1 when this option is selected. When set to 1, any changes made to the current configuration are saved when Windows is closed.
MinOnRun=	Indicates whether the Minimize on Use option of the Program Manager Options menu is selected. This value is 1 when this option is selected. When set to 1, Program Manager is automatically minimized when you run another application.
AutoArrange=	Indicates whether the AutoArrange option of the Program Manager Options menu is selected. This value is 1 when this option is selected. When set to 1, group icons and program items are automatically arranged when you run Program Manager.
Startup=	Specifies the name of the group that serves as the startup group. When this entry is blank, the default program group, StartUp, is used as the startup group.

The [groups] section lists the group files for the Program Manager program groups and describes the order in which they are arranged in the Program Manager window. The [groups] section has two types of entries as listed in Table 9.2.

Table 9.2   The PROGMAN.INI [groups] Section

Entry	Description
Groupx=	Specifies the full path and filename of the group (.GRP) file for a program group. The PROGMAN.INI file contains the same number of Groupx entries as there are program groups and group files. These entries are listed as Group1, Group2, Group3, and so forth.
Order=	Specifies the order of the program groups in the Program Manager window.

If you like the way you have Program Manager configured and don't want anyone to modify it, you can add a section to the PROGMAN.INI file that restricts what can be done to Program Manager. To add restrictions to PROGMAN.INI, add the following section at the end of the file:

[restrictions]

After the [restrictions] heading, you can add any or all of the entries defined in Table 9.3 for access restrictions.

Table 9.3   The PROGMAN.INI [restrictions] Section

Restriction Line	Description
NoSaveSettings =	Prevents the user from selecting Save Settings when exiting Windows.
EditLevel =	This entry can be set to 0, 1, 2, 3, 4 as follows:
	0 Allows the user to make any change.
	1 Prevents the user from creating, deleting, or renaming groups.
	2 Sets the restrictions in EditLevel=1 plus prevents the user from creating or deleting program items.
	3 Sets the restrictions in EditLevel=2 plus prevents the user from changing command lines in a program item.
	4 Sets the restrictions in EditLevel=3 plus prevents the user from changing any program item information.
NoRun = 1	Disables the Run command from the File menu.
NoFileMenu = 1	Disables and removes the File menu.
NoClose = 1	Prevents the user from closing Windows without rebooting.

From Here...

Now that you know how to use Program Manager to manage your applications, program groups, and program items, you are ready to learn how to use File Manager for effective system management.

- Chapter 10, "Using File Manager," explains how you manage your files.

- Chapter 11, "Using the Control Panel," teaches you how to remove drivers and fonts.

- Chapter 12, "Working with Initialization Files," explains how you edit and manage your initialization files.

Chapter 10

Using File Manager

File Manager is a system management tool. It helps you view and organize the files and directories on your system. This chapter provides detailed information on how you can use File Manager to effectively manage your system files and directories. File Manager plays a very important part in the uninstall process because it is the primary tool that you use to locate and remove application files.

In this chapter, you learn to

- Use File Manager to manage your system files and directories

- Use File Manager to uninstall programs and to clean up your system

- Delete and move files and directories

- Locate a file by its name

- Review and edit WINFILE.INI

- Customize File Manager

This chapter explains how to use the Windows 3.1 and Windows for Workgroups File Manager. Windows 95 uses My Computer for basic file browsing and file management. Windows 95 also provides the Windows Explorer for advanced file management. You will also find the Windows 3.1 File Manager in Windows 95; therefore, the procedures in this chapter can be used with Windows 95.

Note

The screen shots used in this chapter were taken from Windows for Workgroups 3.11. If you have Windows 3.1, your File Manager may look a little different. The procedures used in this chapter, however, can be used with Windows 3.1 or Windows for Workgroups.

Managing Your System with File Manager

File Manager is a system management tool. It provides the tools that you need to organize your files and directories. File Manager is a very useful tool during your normal workday. However, it is a vital tool during uninstall and system cleanup sessions. Let's look at how you can use File Manager for these two tasks.

File Manager plays an important part of the overall uninstall process introduced in Chapter 4, "Learning the Uninstall Process," because it allows you to view, locate, and delete application files and directories. File Manager provides the tools you need to remove applications effectively.

During the uninstall process, you will use the various features of File Manager to make backups of your files, create temporary directories, locate files, delete files and directories, view file information, and much more. In this chapter, you'll learn how to perform basic File Manager functions so that you can locate and safely remove application files.

File Manager is very useful during system cleanup. During the system cleanup process, you will need to browse through your directories, then locate and delete any unneeded, temporary, and duplicate files. File Manager provides the fundamental capabilities you need to clean up your system. In this chapter, you'll learn how to use File Manager to perform system cleanup functions.

Understanding Files and Directories

Before we get into the specifics of using File Manager for uninstall and system cleanup sessions, let's review the basics of files and directories.

Computers store information in the form of files. A file can contain an application program, program data, image information, or some other type of information. In Chapter 3, "The Many Types of Files," you saw that Windows works with many different types of files. Your computer system stores files in directories. A directory contains files and sometimes other directories.

In order to keep track of the position of each file and directory on your hard drive, your computer keeps track of the path of each file. The path is a complete description of the location of a file using the following format:

[drive letter]:\[subdirectory]\[additional subdirectories...]\filename.extension

For example, the path C:\WINDOWS\SYSTEM\ARIAL.TTF indicates the following:

- The file is on the C drive

- The file is in the SYSTEM subdirectory of the WINDOWS directory

- The filename is ARIAL.TTF

The path of a file is very important to you and your computer. Without knowing the path of a file, you are unable to locate the file and, therefore, unable to perform any operations on the file.

Another term that you should be familiar with is the root directory. Every drive has a root directory. The root directory for your C drive is C:\. This root directory usually contains files and additional directories. The root directory of your boot drive contains the files that your system needs to boot.

Now that you have reviewed the basics of files and directories, let's look at some of the ways that you can use File Manager to manage your system. The remainder of this chapter provides detailed procedures that you can use with File Manager during uninstall and cleanup sessions.

Sorting Files

File Manager provides several options on how the files on the right side of the directory window are displayed and sorted. During the uninstall process, you can use File Manager's sort options to help you locate and delete application files. You can display files in Program Manager sorted by:

- Filename

- File type

- File size

- File date

To select a particular type of viewing option, select the appropriate menu item from File Manager's Yiew menu. The file sorting options can be very useful depending on your goal. Let's look at how each of these options can help you.

Sorting by Filename

When you choose to sort by filename, it is easy to find a file when you know the filename. For example, if you are looking for a file named TANK.DAT, you would scroll down the file list to the T's until you found the file. Figure 10.1 shows a directory window sorted by filename. Note that files beginning with numbers are listed before files beginning with characters.

> **Note**
>
> No matter which method of file sorting you choose, the subdirectory icons will always appear at the top of the file listing.

Fig. 10.1

Using File Manager's Sort by Name option.

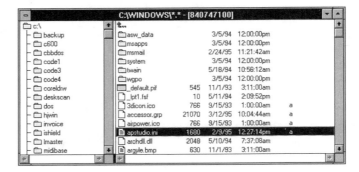

Sorting by File Type

When you select the Sort by Type option, File Manager sorts the files according to their file extension. Sorting by file type is very useful when you are trying to locate particular types of files. For example, let's say you want to locate all of the .DOC files on your system so that you can review them and delete any files that you no longer use or need.

If you select the Sort by Type option, all the .DOC files will be displayed in a group in the file list. Each group of file types is displayed in alphabetical order, therefore, all .DOC files will be displayed before the .GRP files. Figure 10.2 shows a display window with its entries displayed by file type.

Fig. 10.2

Using File Manager's Sort by Type option.

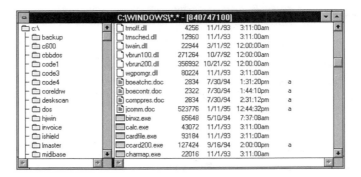

Sorting by File Size

You may find it beneficial to sort your files by their size. This is especially true during system cleanup. After all, deleting one large file can free up as much disk space as dozens of smaller files. When you are cleaning up your system and looking for extraneous files to delete, choose this option and look at the files that are taking up the most space. You make a lot of headway in a short time this way. Figure 10.3 shows a directory window with its contents sorted by file size. Note that the largest files are displayed at the top of the file list.

> **Note**
>
> Just by performing the screen dump in Figure 10.3, I quickly found two files that I no longer needed (the fighters.scr and jcomm.doc files). Deleting these files freed almost 2 MB of disk space. Not bad for a few seconds of work.

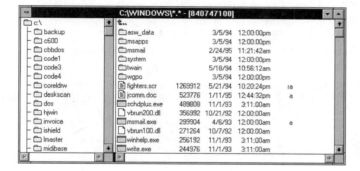

Fig. 10.3
Using File Manager's Sort by Size option.

Sorting by File Date

Sorting by date is another option that you may find useful. Let's say its the end of the year and you've performed a backup of all your data files. You want to clean up your system and start a new year. Sorting by date allows you to quickly locate the old data files so that you can remove them. Figure 10.4 shows a directory window with its file list sorted by date. Note that the newest files are displayed at the top of the list.

Viewing File Properties

File Manager allows you to control the type of file information that is displayed in the directory window's file list. The type of file information that you can control and display includes:

- The filename
- The file size

Tip
Don't make the mistake of thinking that old files are no longer needed and can be deleted. Many of the files used by Windows have dates going back to 1993 and beyond.

■ The date and time the file was last modified

■ The file attributes

Fig. 10.4
Using File
Manager's Sort
by Date option.

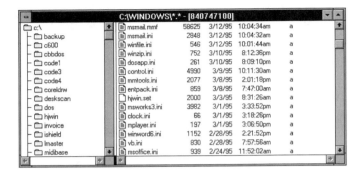

As a minimum, File Manager displays files in the file list by their name. As a maximum, File Manager displays the filename, file size, last modification date, last modification time, and file attributes. The File Manager's View menu can be used to control the combination of file properties that are displayed in the file list. All the figures in this chapter display all the file property information in the directory window.

> **Note**
>
> File attributes include a (for archive file), r (for read-only file), s (for system file), and h (for hidden file). A file may contain any or all of these attributes.

Deleting Files

Tip
Simply click a file to select a single file. To select one or more non-contiguous files, hold down the Ctrl key and click each file. To select a block of contiguous files, hold down the Shift key and click the first and last files in the block.

During uninstall and cleanup sessions, your primary goal is to delete files. Use extreme care whenever you delete files and follow these simple steps:

1. Open File Manager. Click the drive icon for the drive that contains the files you want to delete.

2. Select the appropriate directory from the directory tree on the left side of the directory window.

3. Find and select the file or files that you want to delete from the file list.

4. Choose File, Delete from the File Manager menu or simply press the Del key. Windows will ask you to confirm the delete operation.

5. Choose Yes if you want to provide confirmation for each selected file or choose Yes to All to delete all selected files without confirmation.

All in all, it's a pretty easy procedure for something that can totally wreck your system. So let's be careful out there!

> **Note**
>
> You can easily recover deleted files using File Manager's Undelete feature. If you accidentally delete a file, choose File, Undelete and provide the first letter of the deleted file. The success of the Undelete feature depends on a number of factors. However, as a general rule, undelete a file immediately after deleting it. If you delete a file and then quit Windows, you cannot recover that file when you restart Windows.

Deleting Directories

There may be times when you want to delete an entire directory. This is especially true when you are removing application directories during an uninstall session. Be extremely careful when deleting directories because all files in the directory are also deleted. Follow these simple steps to delete a directory:

1. Open File Manager. Click the drive icon for the drive that contains the files that you want to delete.

2. Select the appropriate directory from the directory tree on the left side of the directory window. Single click the appropriate directory icon to select it.

3. Choose File, Delete from the File Manager menu or simply press the Del key. Windows asks you to confirm the delete operation.

4. Choose Yes if you want to provide confirmation for each file in the directory before it is deleted, or choose Yes to All to delete all files in the directory without confirmation.

> **Caution**
>
> Deleting a directory also deletes all the files and subdirectories in that directory. Review all the files in the directory and in any subdirectories before you delete an entire directory.

Tip
Deleting a directory is the easy way to delete a lot of files. If you want to delete all the files in a directory with the exception of a few, you can move the files you want to save to another directory.

Copying Files

During the uninstall and cleanup process, you will need to make copies of some files—especially your initialization files. With File Manager, you can copy files between disks or between directories on the same disk.

Note

File Manager will either copy or move files depending on the locations of the original and source directories. If you drag-and-drop a file to another directory on the same drive, File Manager moves the file to the new directory. If you drag-and-drop a file to another drive, File Manager creates a copy of the file on the destination drive.

To copy files to another disk, follow these steps:

1. Open File Manager and click the drive icon for the drive that contains the file you want to copy.

2. Select the appropriate directory from the directory tree on the left side of the directory window. Single click the appropriate directory icon to select it.

3. Locate the file you want to copy from the right side of the directory window. Drag-and-drop the file to the appropriate drive icon found on File Manager's drive bar.

   Note

   File Manager copies a file to the current directory on the destination drive. Before you start the copy procedure, make sure that the current directory for the destination drive is the directory where you want the copied file placed. To change the current directory for the destination drive, simply click the appropriate drive icon, then click the appropriate directory from the left side of the directory window. Then proceed with Step 1.

4. File Manager will ask you to confirm the copy operation. Choose Yes to copy the file.

   Caution

   Do not use File Manager's drag-and-drop feature to copy files between directories on the same drive. The file will not be copied to the new directory; it will be moved. The file will removed from the source directory and placed in the destination directory.

To copy files to another location on the same disk, follow these steps:

1. Open File Manager. Click the drive icon for the drive that contains the file that you want to copy.

2. Select the appropriate directory from the directory tree on the left side of the directory window. Single click the appropriate directory icon to select it.

3. Locate the file that you want to copy from the right side of the directory window. Select the file by clicking once on the file.

4. Choose File, Copy from the File Manager menu bar, or press F8. The Copy dialog box is displayed as shown in Figure 10.5.

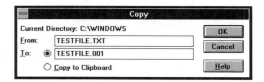

Fig. 10.5
The Copy
dialog box.

5. In the To edit field, type the complete path and filename of the destination file. If you want to simply copy the file to another directory, type the path of the destination directory followed by the original filename—for example, C:\MYAPPS\TESTFILE.TXT. If you want to copy the file using a different filename, type the path of the destination directory followed by the new filename—for example, C:\MYAPPS\TESTFILE.001. If you do not specify a path, the file is copied to the same directory as the source file. In this case, you must use a different filename because File Manager will not overwrite the source file.

6. File Manager asks you to confirm any operation that results in copying over (overwriting) an existing file.

Now that you know how to copy files, let's look at how you can move files and directories.

Moving Files and Directories

File Manager provides an easy way for you to rearrange and organize the files on your hard drive. Using your mouse, you can drag-and-drop files, and even entire directories, to new locations on the hard drive. This is very useful when you need to save all or some of the information in certain files and directories during your uninstall and cleanup sessions. Remember that the File Manager Move feature is available only when moving files and directories to the same drive.

To move files, follow these simple steps:

1. Open File Manager. Click the drive icon for the drive that contains the file(s) you want to move.

2. Select the appropriate directory from the directory tree on the left side of the directory window. Single click the appropriate directory icon to select it.

3. Locate and select the file(s) that you want to copy from the right side of the directory window.

4. Drag-and-drop the file(s) to the appropriate directory icon on the left side of the directory window.

5. File Manager will ask you to confirm the move operation. Choose Yes to move the files.

To move an entire directory (including all its files and subdirectories), follow these steps:

1. Open File Manager. Click the drive icon for the drive that contains the file(s) you want to move.

2. Select the root level directory icon (for example C:\) found at the top of the directory tree on the left side of the directory window. Single click the icon to select it. All the directories located on the disk are displayed on the right side of the directory window.

3. Select the directory that you want to move. Simply click the directory icon to select it.

4. Drag-and-drop the selected directory to the appropriate directory icon on the left side of the directory window. For example, if you wanted to make your MYAPPS directory a subdirectory of the WINDOWS directory, you would drag-and-drop your MYAPPS directory icon from the right side of the directory window to the WINDOWS directory icon on the left side of the directory window.

5. File Manager will ask you to confirm the move operation. Choose Yes to move the directory and all of its files and subdirectories.

Locating Files

Have you ever been in this situation? You know you have something but you forgot where you put it. This happens even when you use your computer. You know that your system contains a file—you even know its name—but you can't find it in any directory. Fortunately, File Manager provides a neat little feature that searches your hard drive and locates your missing file.

File Manager's Search feature allows you to locate a specific file on your hard drive. This feature is really useful when you are cleaning your system and removing stray application files. To use the Search feature, follow these steps:

1. Open File Manager. Click the drive icon for the drive that contains the file that you are trying to locate.

2. Choose File, Search from the File Manager menu bar. The Search dialog box is displayed as shown in Figure 10.6.

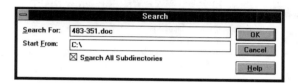

Fig. 10.6
The Search dialog box.

3. In the Search For edit field, enter the name of the file that you are trying to locate.

4. In the Start From edit field, enter the path of the directory from where you want to begin the search. As a general rule, use the root level directory for the drive (for example, C:\).

5. Click the Search All Subdirectories check box. This way, the entire directory structure will be searched. If you do not check this box, only the top-level directories in the directory tree will be searched.

6. Click the OK button to execute the search. File Manager displays a status dialog box that indicates the progress of the search.

When File Manager has completed the search, the Search Results dialog box will be displayed as shown in Figure 10.7. The information in the Search Results dialog box indicates the path of the file and additional file information. You can use the path information to locate the file.

Tip
You can use DOS wildcards in the Search For edit field. For example, typing *.doc in the edit field causes File Manager to generate a complete list of all the files on the drive that contain the .DOC file extension.

Fig. 10.7
The Search Results dialog box.

Understanding WINFILE.INI

The WINFILE.INI file is the initialization file used by File Manager. This file contains information that File Manager uses to configure itself. WINFILE.INI contains only one section, [settings]. The [settings] section contains the entries listed in Table 10.1. You can use the entries in WINFILE.INI to customize the File Manager to suit your tastes and needs.

Table 10.1	Entries for the [settings] Section of WINFILE.INI
Entry	**Description**
ConfirmDelete=	Indicates whether the user is prompted for confirmation when deleting a file. This value is 1 to enable confirmation.
ConfirmFormat=	Indicates whether the user is prompted for confirmation when formatting a disk. This value is 1 to enable confirmation.
ConfirmMouse=	Indicates whether the user is prompted for confirmation during drag-and-drop operations. This value is 1 to enable confirmation.
ConfirmReplace=	Indicates whether the user is prompted for confirmation when overwriting a file. This value is 1 to enable confirmation.
ConfirmSubDel=	Indicates whether the user is prompted for confirmation when deleting a subdirectory. This value is 1 to enable confirmation.
dir1=	Specifies the current directory settings
Face=	Specifies the typeface used for desktop item. The Small Fonts typeface is used by default.
LowerCase=	Indicates whether files appear in lowercase. This value is 1 when the files appear in lowercase.
Size=	Specifies the typeface size. The default size is 8.
Window=	Specifies the size and position of the windows as well as the state (maximized, minimized, restored) when opened.

Table 10.1 lists several entries that are used for confirmation purposes. If you want to change these values, you can do so through the File Manager menu. Choose Options, Confirmation to select the confirmation options that you desire.

From Here...

Now that you know how to use File Manager to manage your system's files and directories, you are ready to learn how to use the Windows Control Panel to manage your system's configuration.

- Chapter 11, "Using the Control Panel," teaches you how to remove drivers and fonts.

- Chapter 12, "Working with Initialization Files," explains how you edit and manage your initialization files.

- Chapter 13, "Uninstalling Microsoft Office: A Sample Uninstall Session," takes you step-by-step through a complete uninstall session.

Chapter 11

Using the Control Panel

The Windows Control Panel is a configuration management tool that allows you to interface with configuration management utilities called *applets*. These applets allow you to control many aspects of the Windows environment from the appearance of the Windows desktop to the configuration of your multimedia hardware.

In this chapter, you learn to

- Use the Control Panel
- Recognize the different types of font files
- Use the Printers applet to control your printer drivers
- Recognize the different types of drivers and their uses
- Review and edit the Control Panel initialization file, CONTROL.INI

This chapter explains how to use the Windows 3.1 and Windows for Workgroups Control Panel. Windows 95 also provides a Control Panel. Refer to your Windows 95 documentation for information on the procedures you need to use with Windows 95.

Reviewing the Control Panel

Windows provides the Control Panel as your primary interface to your system, system drivers, and configuration settings. During the uninstall process, you will need to use various features of the Control Panel to remove drivers, fonts, and more.

The Control Panel, as shown in Figure 11.1, contains icons that represent utilities, called applets, that allow you to control the configuration of your system. Each applet performs a certain function. Table 11.1 lists the applets that you are most likely to find in your Control Panel. Of course, the actual applets you will find depends on your hardware and system. Many hardware vendors provide applets that allow you to configure the hardware once you have installed it on your system. Figure 11.1 shows the Set Res applet (provided by the manufacturer of my display adapter) that is used to set the resolution of the display adapter.

Fig. 11.1
The Windows
Control Panel.

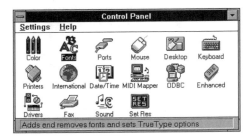

Table 11.1	**Common Control Panel Applets**	
Applet Icon	**Name**	**Description**
Enhanced	386 Enhanced	Controls the 386 enhanced features of Windows including virtual memory and swapfile settings.
Color	Color	Controls the color scheme Windows uses to color application windows.
Date/Time	Date/Time	Sets the system date and time.
Desktop	Desktop	Controls the appearance of the Windows desktop including the background pattern, the wallpaper, and screensaver.
Drivers	Drivers	Adds, removes, and configures device drivers (primarily multimedia drivers).
Fonts	Fonts	Adds and removes fonts.
Keyboard	Keyboard	Controls parameters for the keyboard including repeat key rate and delay.
Mouse	Mouse	Controls parameters for the mouse including the acceleration, double-click speed, and sensitivity.
Ports	Ports	Specifies the parameters for the serial communications ports.

Applet Icon	Name	Description
 Printers	Printers	Adds, removes, and configures printer drivers.
 Sound	Sound	Assigns sounds to Windows events.

Although not all of the applets are important to effective configuration management, we're going to look at several applets that are a crucial part of the overall uninstall process. In this chapter, we take a close look at the following Control Panel applets:

■ The Fonts applet

■ The Printers applet

■ The Drivers applet

These Control Panel applets play an important role in two phases of configuration management: uninstalling applications and cleaning up your system.

Uninstalling Applications with the Control Panel

The Control Panel plays an important part of the overall uninstall process outlined in this book because it controls much of Windows configuration. The role of the Control Panel during the uninstall process varies depending on the type of application you are uninstalling. Let's look at a few uninstall examples to demonstrate the role of the Control Panel applets in the uninstall process.

■ **Example 1:** You are uninstalling a computer-aided design (CAD) application from your machine. You used the CAD application for a design project and you no longer need it. The CAD application was used with a networked plotter for output. No other applications use the network plotter or the fonts provided with the CAD application.

In this case, you need to remove the CAD application files, the CAD program group, the plotter driver, and the fonts used by the CAD application and plotter. The Control Panel applets must be used to complete this uninstall process. The Fonts applet is used to remove the fonts. The Printers applet is used to remove the plotter driver.

- **Example 2:** You are uninstalling an image-processing application that interfaces with your color scanner. The project is over and you are permanently removing your scanner and your image-processing application. The application has installed several dozen fonts on your system. Some of them you would like to keep while you want to get rid of others.

  In this case, you need to remove the application files, the application program group, the scanner driver, and some of the fonts. The Control Panel Fonts applet is used in this case to remove the fonts. You may think that you would use the Drivers applet to remove the scanner driver. This is not the case. The way that you remove the scanner driver depends on how the scanner interfaces with your system. Most scanners are SCSI devices and have drivers that are loaded during startup in the AUTOEXEC.BAT or CONFIG.SYS file.

- **Example 3:** You are uninstalling an old version of a word processor. The word processor uses the same printer as your new word processor and you want to keep all the fonts that you have on your system.

  In this case, all you have to do is remove the application files and the application program group. You don't have to use the Control Panel applets in this situation.

As you can see in the previous three examples, the role of Control Panel applets in the uninstall process really depends on the situation. Now let's see how you can use the Control Panel for cleaning up your system.

Cleaning Up Your System with the Control Panel

The Control Panel offers several applets you can use to review and clean up your system. The following briefly describes the applets that you use when cleaning up your system:

- The Fonts applet allows you to add and remove fonts and, optionally, font files from your system. Use the Fonts applet to periodically review the fonts that are installed on your system. Remove the fonts that you don't use and delete any font files that are not needed.

- The Printers applet allows you to add, remove, and configure printer drivers. During system cleanup, review the installed list of printer drivers and remove the printer drivers that you don't need.

■ The Drivers applet is used to add and remove various device drivers including multimedia drivers. Review this section periodically for unnecessary and unused drivers.

The remainder of this chapter provides detailed information on how you can use each of these Control Panel applets to clean up your system.

Using the Fonts Applet

Fonts are really cool! With fonts, you can change ordinary text into spectacular presentations. Today's word-processing and presentation graphics applications provide you with enough fonts to choke a horse—well, maybe not a horse, but definitely Windows. Applications like CorelDRAW! (CD-ROM version) install hundreds of fonts on your system. Although this seems great, fonts require a good deal of overhead: they use system resources, increase the amount of time that it takes Windows to start, and slow down some applications.

Most users will never use all the fonts that come with today's applications. Fortunately, Windows provides a convenient way to manage your system fonts—the Control Panel Fonts applet as shown in Figure 11.2. This applet allows you to add fonts, delete fonts, and set TrueType options. Before we get into the actual steps for using the Fonts applet, let's take a closer look at what fonts are and how Windows uses them.

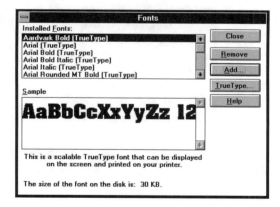

Fig. 11.2
The Fonts dialog box.

Learning about Fonts

Windows uses fonts to display and print text. A font is a collection of characters that have common characteristics. Fonts are characterized by the typeface, size, and style. The typeface refers to the overall appearance of the font.

Courier, Times New Roman, and Arial are examples of typefaces. Font styles refer to variations in a typeface such as bold, underlined, and italics. Fonts are sized by the point. One point is equal to 1/72 of an inch. Therefore, a font with a point size of 18 is 18/72, or 1/4, inches high.

Windows supports a number of different types of fonts. The three primary types of user fonts that Windows supports are raster, vector, and TrueType fonts as described in Chapter 3, "The Many Types of Files."

Table 11.2 lists the raster fonts installed with Windows 3.1.

Table 11.2 Raster Fonts Provided with Windows 3.1	
Raster Font Filename	**Font Name**
COURIER.FON	Courier
SSERIFx.FON	MS Sans Serif
SERIFx.FON	MS Serif
SMALLx.FON	Small
SYMBOLx.FON	Symbol

Note

The x suffix in the filenames indicates that the filename contains a letter that specifies the resolution of the raster font. An A suffix indicates CGA resolution; B is EGA resolution; C is 60 by 72 dpi printer resolution; D is 120 by 72 dpi printer resolution; E is VGA resolution; F is 8514/A resolution. For example, the SMALLA.FON file is designed for the CGA screen resolution.

Table 11.3 lists the TrueType fonts provided with Windows 3.1.

Table 11.3 TrueType Fonts Provided with Windows 3.1	
TrueType Filenames	**Font Name**
ARIAL.TTF, ARIAL.FOT	Arial
ARIALBD.TTF, ARIALBD.FOT	Arial Bold
ARIALBI.TTF, ARIALBI,FOT	Arial Bold Italic
ARIALI.TTF, ARIALI.FOT	Arial Italic

TrueType Filenames	Font Name
COUR.TTF, COUR.FOT	Courier
COURBD.TTF, COURBD.FOT	Courier Bold
COURBI.TTF, COURBI.FOT	Courier Bold Italic
COURI.TTF, COURI.FOT	Courier Italic
TIMES.TTF, TIMES.FOT	Times New Roman
TIMESBD.TTF, TIMESBD.FOT	Times New Roman Bold
TIMESBI.TTF, TIMESBI.FOT	Times New Roman Bold Italic
TIMESI.TTF, TIMESI.FOT	Times New Roman Italic
SYMBOL.TTF, SYMBOL.FOT	Symbol
WINGDING.TTF, WINGDING.FOT	Wingding

Windows also works with one other type of font: system fonts. System fonts are used internally by Windows for various displays. Table 11.4 lists the three system fonts supplied by Windows.

Table 11.4 Windows System Fonts	
Font	**Description**
System	Used to draw menus, dialog box controls, and other text.
Fixed	Used for backwards-compatibility with Windows 2.x and earlier versions of Windows. This is a fixed-width font.
OEM, or Terminal	Supports OEM text copied to the clipboard viewer from Windows and DOS applications. This is a fixed-width font.

Now that you are familiar with fonts, let's look at the ways you can use the Fonts applet to manage the fonts on your system.

Removing Fonts

You can remove fonts currently installed in Windows using the Control Panel Fonts applet. Removing fonts that you don't use frees Windows memory and, optionally, disk space. When you remove a font from Windows, you are removing the font from the Windows list of installed fonts. You are not actually removing the font from your hard drive. You can, however, remove both fonts and font files using the options provided by the Fonts applet. To remove fonts (and, optionally, font files), follow these simple steps:

1. Open the Control Panel and double-click the Fonts icon. The Fonts dialog box is displayed (refer to Fig. 11.2).

2. Select one or more fonts that you want to use from the Installed Fonts list box.

3. Click the Remove button once you have selected the font(s) you want to remove. The Remove Font dialog box is displayed as shown in Figure 11.3.

Fig. 11.3
The Remove Font
dialog box.

4. If you want to remove the font files from your hard drive, click the Delete Font File From Disk check box.

> **Caution**
>
> Be careful when deleting font files from the source disk. If you are using fonts that are located on a network drive, do not click the Delete Font File From Disk check box. Doing so will remove the font files from the network drive, making the font unavailable to all users.

5. Click the Remove button to remove one font at a time, or click the Remove All button to remove all the selected fonts. After all the fonts have been removed, you will be taken back to the Fonts dialog box. From the Fonts dialog box, you can then remove more fonts, add fonts, set TrueType options, or close the Fonts applet.

Deleting Font Files

As part of system cleanup, remove font files that you don't need. Most font files are found in the WINDOWS and WINDOWS/SYSTEM directories and have the .FON, .FOT, or .TTF file extensions. Most font files have a name that indicates the family name, or typeface, of the font. For example, COUR.TTF is the standard Courier TrueType font, COURBD.TTF is the bold Courier font, and COURI.TTF is the italic Courier font. Before you go on a search and destroy mission, review and follow these steps.

1. Use the Fonts applet to determine which fonts are currently being used by Windows. Make a note of which files are currently installed. If you find fonts that you don't use, remove those fonts.

2. Use File Manager to view the files of your WINDOWS and WINDOWS/SYSTEM directory.

3. Locate the font files (.FON, .FOT, and .TTF files) in these directories and compare these font files with your list of installed font files. Determine which font files do not match your list of installed fonts. Make a note of the files that you may want to delete.

4. Compare your list of possible font files to delete with the lists of font files provided in Tables 11.2, 11.3, and 11.4. It is probably safe to delete a file if you can't find a matching installed font or font file from the tables in this chapter. See Chapter 10, "Using File Manager," for the steps you need to delete these files.

Tip

When you are trying to identify font files that are being used by your system, look in the WIN.INI file under the [fonts] section. The entries in this section list the filenames of the font files being used by the system.

Using the Printers Applet

Windows uses printer drivers to communicate with the printer(s) connected to your system. A printer driver is special software that translates Windows device-independent information into data that the printer can understand. The printer driver also allows Windows to take full advantage of the features of the printer including printer fonts and resources.

The Control Panel Printers applet, as shown in Figure 11.4, allows you to install, update, and delete printer drivers. Whenever a new printer is made available to your system, whether through a direct connection or network connection, you must install a new printer driver. Likewise, whenever a printer is no longer accessible to your system, remove the associated printer driver.

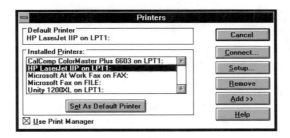

Fig. 11.4
The Printers applet.

In an effort to manage your system, you need to know how to remove printer drivers and delete printer driver files from your system.

Removing Printer Drivers

Having unused printer drivers is a waste of system resources. As you are cleaning up your system, review your list of installed printer drivers and remove those that are not needed. The following steps can be used to remove printer drivers:

1. Open the Control Panel and double-click the Printers icon. The Printers dialog box is displayed (refer to Fig. 11.4).

2. Select the printer driver that you want to remove from the Installed Printers list box.

3. Once you have selected the printer, click the Remove button. You will be asked to confirm the removal of the printer driver.

4. After you have removed all the printer drivers that you want to remove, click OK.

> **Note**
>
> When you remove a printer from the Windows list of installed printers, you are not removing the printer driver file from your hard drive. You are merely keeping Windows from loading the driver into memory and making that driver available to your applications. The following section provides more information about deleting printer driver files.

Deleting Printer Driver Files

As you install and remove printer drivers, you will inadvertently leave unused printer driver files on your system. If you bought your system with Windows already installed, you probably have dozens of unnecessary drivers on your system because hardware vendors typically copy every possible driver (printer, display, multimedia, and so forth) that you might use on to the system.

Tip
To identify printer driver files that are being used by your system, look in the CONTROL.INI file under the [Installed] section. The entries in this section list the filenames of the printer drivers being used by the system.

When you are performing a cleanup of your system, you need to review your printer drivers and delete those that you don't need. To review and delete printer driver files, follow these steps:

1. Use the Printers applet to determine which printer drivers are currently being used by Windows. Make a note of which drivers are currently installed. If you find printer drivers that you don't use, review the previous section, "Removing Printer Drivers," to remove the drivers.

2. Use File Manager to view the files of your WINDOWS and WINDOWS/SYSTEM directory.

3. Locate the printer driver files (usually with .DRV file extensions) in these directories and compare these driver files with your list of installed printer files.

4. Determine which printer driver files do not match your list of installed printers. Make a note of the files that you may want to delete.

> **Caution**
>
> Be careful when deleting a printer driver file because most printer driver files contain printer drivers for more than one printer. For example, if you have upgraded from an HP Laserjet II and an HP Laserjet IV printer, you wouldn't want to delete any printer driver with HP in the name. The printer driver file might contain the drivers for both printers. Deleting the file for the HP Laserjet II may also delete the printer driver for your new HP Laserjet IV.

5. It is safe to delete a printer driver file if you can't find a match in the list of installed printers.

> **Note**
>
> If you want to be safe before deleting a printer driver file, move all of the printer driver files you want to delete to a new directory called PRINTERS. Use your computer for a few days and if all of your printers are available and working, it is safe to delete the printer driver files in the PRINTERS directory.

Tip

You can usually determine the manufacturer of a driver file by looking at the filename. The filename usually contains the name (or an abbreviation for the name) of the printer manufacturer. For example, Sound Blaster drivers have SB in the filename.

Using the Drivers Applet

Device drivers are a crucial part of your system. Windows uses device drivers to communicate with the various peripherals attached to your system including the mouse, keyboard, and display adapter. Windows provides several ways to install device drivers on your system.

During installation, Windows automatically installs the mouse, keyboard, and display adapter device drivers. As we saw in the previous section of this chapter, printer drivers are installed using the Control Panel Printers applet. Most other device drivers, however, are installed through the Control Panel Drivers applet as shown in Figure 11.5.

Fig. 11.5

The Drivers applet.

Before getting into the procedures you use to remove and delete device drivers, let's learn a little more about device drivers.

Learning about Device Drivers

Windows supports many different types of device drivers. The following are the most common types:

- Display drivers

- Mouse drivers

- Keyboard drivers

- Printer drivers

- Communications drivers

- Multimedia drivers

- System drivers

- Network drivers

- Virtual device drivers

Let's take a closer look at each of these types of drivers. As you review these driver types, pay particular attention to how these drivers are added to and removed from your system. Most of these driver types are installed when Windows is installed.

The Windows Setup program in the Main program group can be used to change the driver types that are installed during the Windows Setup process (display drivers, network drivers, mouse drivers, and keyboard drivers). The Control Panel Drivers applet is primarily used to add and remove multimedia drivers.

Display Drivers

Display drivers are used to support your system's display adapter. When you install Windows, Windows determines the capabilities of your adapter and installs a compatible display driver. Windows typically installs the VGA display driver. This driver supports 640 by 480 resolution in 16 colors. Most display adapters shipped over the past few years support the VGA display mode. However, the display adapter on your system probably supports higher resolutions and more colors.

To take full advantage of your display adapter's capabilities, you need to install a new display driver. The display drivers for your adapter were most likely provided on a floppy disk along with your adapter card or system. To install the new display adapter, you need to run the Windows Setup routine from the Main program group. The Control Panel Drivers applet is not used to install display drivers. Table 11.5 lists the display drivers provided with Windows 3.1.

Tip

When you are performing system cleanup, determine which display adapter your system uses and remove the others from your hard drive. The display drivers are typically found in the WINDOWS/SYSTEM directory.

Table 11.5 Display Drivers Provided with Windows 3.1	
Driver File	**Display Adapter**
8514.DRV	8514/A Adapter
EGA.DRV	EGA Adapter
EGAHIBW.DRV	EGA Adapter with 128K RAM
EGAMONO.DRV	EGA Monochrome Adapter
HERCULES.DRV	Hercules Monochrome Adapter
MMTLHI.DRV	ET4000 Adapter (large fonts)
MMTLLO.DRV	ET4000 Adapter (small fonts)
OLIBW.DRV	Olivetti/AT&T Monochrome or PVC Adapter
PLASMA.DRV	COMPAQ Portable Plasma Adapter
SUPERVGA.DRV	Super VGA Adapter
TIGA.DRV	TIGA Adapter
VGA.DRV	VGA Adapter
VGAMONO.DRV	VGA Monochrome Adapter
V7VGA.DRV	Video Seven VGA Adapter
XGA.DRV	XGA Adapter

Tip

If you install a new type of mouse, delete the previous mouse driver. The mouse drivers are typically found in the WINDOWS/ SYSTEM directory.

Mouse Drivers

Mouse drivers support the mouse, or other pointing device, that is attached to your system through either an adapter card or a communications port. During installation, Windows usually determines the type of mouse that is attached to your system and automatically loads the proper driver. If you need to install a new mouse driver, or update an existing mouse driver, you must run the Window Setup routine found in the Main program group. The Control Panel Drivers applet is not used to install mouse drivers. Table 11.6 lists the mouse drivers provided with Windows 3.1.

Table 11.6 Mouse Drivers Provided with Windows 3.1	
Driver File	**Mouse Type**
HPMOUSE.DRV	Hewlett-Packard Mouse
LMOUSE.DRV	Logitech Serial Mouse
MSC3BC2.DRV	Mouse Systems COM2/3 Button Mouse
MSCMOUSE.DRV	Mouse Systems Serial/Bus Mouse
MOUSE.DRV	Microsoft Mouse, IBM PS/2 Mouse, Logitech Bus, or Logitech PS/2 Mouse
NOMOUSE.DRV	No Mouse

Keyboard Drivers

A keyboard driver provides the interface between Windows and your keyboard. When Windows is installed, the KEYBOARD.DRV driver is copied to your WINDOWS/SYSTEM directory. This keyboard driver is a standard driver for all Windows systems worldwide. To support international keyboards and languages, Windows uses keyboard tables (in the form of .DLL files) to reference the appropriate language library.

Printer Drivers

Printer drivers allow Windows to communicate with your printer(s) and/or other output device(s). When Windows is installed, it asks you to specify the printers that are available to your system. Windows then installs the appropriate printer drivers. The Control Panel Printers applet allows you to add and remove printer drivers. Refer to "Using the Printers Applet" in this chapter for more information on printer drivers.

Communications Drivers

Windows uses the COMM.DRV communications drivers to handle both serial and parallel device communications.

Caution
Do not remove the COMM.DRV file from your system. Windows will not be able to communicate with your serial or parallel ports if the COMM.DRV file is removed.

Multimedia Drivers

Windows 3.1 supports multimedia devices through its Media Control Interface (MCI). The MCI provides device independence for Windows multimedia applications. Windows applications use MCI commands to access the Windows multimedia capabilities. The multimedia drivers translate the Windows MCI commands into data that the multimedia hardware (CD-ROM drive, audio device, video device, and so on) can understand.

Several of the multimedia drivers provided by Windows are MCI-level drivers. The non-MCI (hardware-specific) multimedia drivers that you need to take advantage of your multimedia hardware are usually provided with your multimedia upgrade kit (or with your system if it came with multimedia capabilities). The Control Panel Drivers applet is used to add and remove multimedia drivers. Table 11.7 lists the multimedia drivers provided with Windows 3.1.

Table 11.7 Multimedia Drivers Provided with Windows 3.1	
Driver File	**Multimedia Driver**
MCICDA.DRV	MCI CD-Audio Driver
MCISEQ.DRV	MCI MIDI Driver
MCIWAVE.DRV	MCI Waveform Audio Driver
MIDIMAP.DRV	MIDI Mapper Control Panel Extension Driver
MMSOUND.DRV	Multimedia Sound Driver
MPU401.DRV	MIDI MPU401-Compatibles Driver
MSADLIB.DRV	MIDI Adlib-Compatibles Driver
SNDBLST.DRV	Sound Blaster 1.5 DSP Driver
SNDBLST2.DRV	Sound Blaster 2.0 DSP Driver
TIMER.DRV	Multimedia Timer Driver

If you remove any multimedia hardware from your system, or don't use the multimedia equipment that you have, go into the Control Panel Drivers applet and remove the drivers that are not currently being used.

> **Note**
>
> Many of the multimedia CD-ROM titles on the market today install several multimedia drivers on your system for video and audio playback. Review the drivers listed from your Drivers applet and determine which drivers you need. The QuickTime, Indeo, and Video for Windows multimedia drivers are used for video playback. You may want to remove these unless you frequently play videos on your system. If you remove them, you can always reinstall them later using the setup routine that came with the multimedia application.

System Drivers

Windows provides two system drivers for system support: SYSTEM.DRV and HPSYSTEM.DRV. These files provide support for the system timer, system disks, and system hooks. The SYSTEM.DRV file is used by Windows to support most systems. The HPSYSTEM.DRV file is used to support the HP Vectra system.

> **Caution**
>
> Do remove the system driver file SYSTEM.DRV or HPSYSTEM.DRV because Windows cannot operate without them.

Network Drivers

The Windows network drivers provide an interface to File Manager, Printer Manager, and the Control Panel. When Windows is installed, the network driver for your network (if any) is installed. If you need to add or update a network driver, the Windows Setup routine in the Main program group must be used. The Control Panel Drivers applet is not used to install or remove network drivers. Table 11.8 lists the network drivers and supporting files provided with Windows 3.1 or Windows for Workgroups.

Table 11.8 Network Driver Files Provided with Windows

Driver File	Network
WFWNET.DRV	Windows for Workgroups network driver
NETAPI.DLL	Windows for Workgroups network API library

Driver File	Network
PMSPL.DLL	Windows for Workgroups printer API library
LMSCRIPT.EXE	LAN Manager script support utility
LMSCRIPT.PIF	LAN Manager PIF file
MSNET.DRV	Generic Network Driver that supports 3Com 3+Share, 3Com 3+Open LAN Manager, Banyan VINES 4.0, Microsoft LAN Manager 1.x, Microsoft LAN Manager 2.0 Basic, Microsoft Network, and IBM PC LAN.
NETWARE.DRV	Novell NetWare 2.10 or above driver
NWPOPUP.EXE	File for pop-up message support
NETX.COM	Workstation shell
ROUTE.COM	Token Ring IPX routing file
MSIPX.COM	NDIS-compliant IPX protocol
MSIPX.SYS	NDIS Shim for MSIPX.COM

Virtual Device Drivers

A virtual driver is a special type of device driver that can be used when Windows is running in 386 enhanced mode. A virtual device driver is a 32-bit protected mode dynamic link library that supports a specific hardware or software resource and manages the resource in such a way that it can be used simultaneously by more than one application.

Windows uses a series of virtual device drivers for enhanced mode operation. Most of the Windows virtual memory support is provided by the WIN386.EXE file. When WIN386.EXE is loaded, it reads the SYSTEM.INI file and loads all the files specified in the [386enh] section. Some of the files in the [386enh] section are internal to the WIN386.EXE file. The other files are found in the WINDOWS\SYSTEM directory. Table 11.9 lists the standard virtual device drivers supplied with Windows and Windows for Workgroups.

> **Note**
>
> You can remove some of the virtual device drivers that are being used by your system to free up hard disk space such as the driver files with the .386 file extension from your WINDOWS\SYSTEM listed in Tables 11.9, 11.10, and 11.11; however, be sure that the files you delete are not listed in the [386enh] section of SYSTEM.INI.

Table 11.9 Virtual Device Drivers for WIN386.EXE Support	
Filename	**Supports**
BANINST.386	Banyan VINES 4.0
DECNB.386	DEC Pathworks
DECNET.386	DECNET
LANMAN10.386	LAN Manager 1.0
HPEBIOS.386	EBIOS for HP machines
LVMD.386	Logitech mouse
MSCVMD.386	Mouse Systems mouse
V7VDD.386	Video 7 display adapters
VADLIBD.386	Adlib and compatible devices
VDD8514.386	8514/A display adapters
VDDCGA.386	CGA display adapters
VDDCT441.386	82C441 VGA display adapters
VDDEGA.386	EGA display adapters
VDDHERC.386	Hercules monochrome adapters
VDDTIGA.386	TIGA display adapters
VDDVGA30.386	VGA display adapters
VDDXGA.386	XGA display adapters
VIPX.386	Novell NetWare IPX
VNETWARE.386	Novell NetWare
VPOWERD.386	Advanced Power Management
VSBD.386	Sound Blaster devices
VTDAPI.386	Multimedia timers

Table 11.10   Virtual Device Drivers for WIN386.EXE Support Provided with Windows for Workgroups 3.1

Filename	Supports
MONOUMB2.386	Monochrome UMB
VCD.386	Communications devices
VDMAD.386	DMA devices
VPD.386	Printer devices
VPICD.386	Programmable interrupt controller devices
VBROWSE.386	WFW network browsing device
VNB.386	WFW NetBEUI device
VNETBIOS.386	WFW NetBIOS device
VNETSUP.386	WFW network support device
VREDIR.386	WFW network redirector
VSERVER.386	WFW network server
VSHARE.386	WFW file sharing device
VWC.386	WFW workgroup client device

Table 11.11   Virtual Device Drivers for WIN386.EXE Support Provided with Windows for Workgroups 3.11

Filename	Supports
IOS.386	I/O supervisor
IFSMGR.386	File system manager
LPT.386	LPT devices
RMM.D32	Real mode disk devices
SERIAL.386	Serial communications devices
VCACHE.386	32-bit cache manager
VCOMM.386	Communications devices

(continues)

Table 11.11 Continued	
Filename	**Supports**
VFAT.386	32-bit FAT devices
VXDLDR.386	Dynamic loaders

Now that you have learned the basic types of drivers, let's look at how you can use the Control Panel Drivers applet to add and remove drivers.

Removing Drivers

Tip
If you always run Windows in 386 enhanced mode, you can delete the KRNL286.EXE file from your WIN-DOWS directory. This file is only needed when you run Windows in standard mode.

As you are cleaning up your system, review your list of installed drivers and remove those that are not needed. The following steps can be used to remove unused multimedia drivers:

1. Open the Control Panel and double-click the Drivers icon. The Drivers dialog box is displayed (refer to Fig. 11.5).

2. Select the driver you want to remove from the Installed Drivers list box.

3. Click the Remove button. You will be asked to confirm the removal of the driver.

4. After you have removed all the drivers that you want to remove, click Close.

> **Note**
>
> Changes made with the Drivers applet may prompt Windows to display a dialog box asking whether or not you want to restart Windows. Restarting Windows frees the memory used by the driver.
>
> When you remove a driver from the Windows list of installed drivers, you are not removing the driver file from your hard drive. You are merely keeping Windows from loading the driver into memory and making that driver available to your applications. The following section provides more information about deleting driver files.

Deleting Driver Files

As you make changes to your multimedia system and its drivers, you will inadvertently leave unused multimedia driver files on your system. If you bought your system with Windows already installed, you probably have dozens of unnecessary drivers on your system because hardware vendors typically copy every possible driver (multimedia, printer, display, and so forth) that you might use onto the system.

When you are performing a cleanup of your system, you need to review your drivers and delete those that you don't need. To review and delete driver files, follow these steps:

1. Use the Drivers applet to determine which multimedia drivers are currently being used by Windows. Make a note of which drivers are currently installed. If you find drivers that you don't use, review the section in this chapter, "Removing Drivers."

2. Use File Manager to view the files in your WINDOWS and WINDOWS/SYSTEM directory.

3. Locate the multimedia driver files (usually with .DRV file extensions) in these directories and compare these driver files with your list of installed multimedia drivers.

4. Determine which driver files do not match your list of installed drivers. Make a note of the files that you may want to delete.

5. It is safe to delete a driver file if you can't find a match in the list of installed drivers. See Chapter 10, "Using File Manager," for the steps you need to delete these files.

> **Caution**
>
> If you want to be safe before deleting a driver file, move all of the driver files that you want to delete to a new directory called DRIVERS. Use your computer for a few days. If everything works okay, it is safe to delete the driver files in the DRIVERS directory.

Understanding CONTROL.INI

As with most Windows applications, the Control Panel has an initialization file associated with it. This file is the CONTROL.INI file and it contains several sections that are used by the various applets in the Control Panel. Table 11.12 lists and describes the various sections of the CONTROL.INI file.

Table 11.12 Sections of the CONTROL.INI File	
Section	**Description**
[Current]	Defines the current color scheme used by Windows to paint the various elements of application windows. This section is used by the Color applet.

(continues)

Tip
When you are trying to identify driver files that are being used by your system, look in the CONTROL.INI file under the [Userinstallable.drivers] and [Drivers.Desc] sections. The entries in these sections list the filenames of the multimedia drivers being used by the system.

Tip
It is a good idea to review the CONTROL.INI file when you are trying to clean up your system. The CONTROL.INI file helps you to identify printer driver files and multimedia driver files that are being used by your system.

Table 11.12 Continued

Section	Description
[Color Schemes]	Specifies the color codes used with each color scheme. Each color code describes the color used for an element of the application window (title bar, background, text, and so forth). This section is used by the Color applet.
[Custom Colors]	Specifies the custom colors selected for the custom palette used by the Color applet.
[Drivers.Desc]	Specifies the filename and descriptions of the installed multimedia drivers. This section is used by the Drivers applet.
[Installed]	Specifies the filenames of the installed printer drivers. This section is used by the Printers applet.
[MMCPL]	Specifies values associated with the multimedia items in the Control Panel.
[Patterns]	Specifies the color values used to create the background pattern for the Windows desktop. This section is used by the Desktop applet.
[Screen Saver.savername]	Specifies the values associated with a particular Windows 3.1-compatible screensaver module. The CONTROL.INI may contain more than one screensaver section. The screensaver sections are distinguished by the savername section heading. These sections are used by the Desktop applet.
[Userinstallable.drivers]	Defines values used by the user-installable multimedia drivers. This section is used by the Drivers applet.

From Here...

Now that you know how to use the Control Panel and some of its applets to add and remove fonts, printers, and drivers, you are ready to learn how to review and modify the Windows and DOS initialization files to clean up, configure, and optimize your system.

- Chapter 12, "Working with Initialization Files," explains how you edit and manage your initialization files.

- Chapter 13, "Uninstalling Microsoft Office: A Sample Uninstall Session," takes you step-by-step through a complete uninstall session.

Chapter 12

Working with Initialization Files

Windows and Windows applications use and store configuration information in special files called initialization files. These files are formatted in such a way that Windows and Windows applications can easily find any needed information. This chapter introduces you to initialization files and provides detailed information on the sections and entries in the most important initialization files, WIN.INI and SYSTEM.INI. During the uninstall process, you will need to review and edit the initialization files to remove information used by the application you are deleting.

In this chapter, you learn to

■ Review and edit initialization files

■ Use SysEdit to edit SYSTEM.INI and WIN.INI

■ Use Notepad to edit initialization files

■ Understand the sections and entries in SYSTEM.INI and WIN.INI

This chapter explains how to work with Windows 3.1 and Windows for Workgroups initialization files. Windows 95 supports Windows 3.1 applications and, therefore, supports initialization files. However, Windows 95 applications use the Windows 95 Registry for storing settings and configuration information. When using Windows 95, you only need to review and edit initialization files when you are removing Windows 3.1 applications. Use the Windows 95 Registry Editor to edit the Windows 95 Registry when removing Windows 95 applications.

Reviewing Initialization Files

An initialization file is a special type of file used by Windows and Windows applications to store various types of information including configurations, settings, passwords, user preferences, and so forth. When Windows is installed, several initialization files are copied to your system. These files are used by Windows and the standard Windows components. Table 12.1 lists the Windows initialization files that are discussed in this book.

Table 12.1	Windows 3.1 Initialization Files
Filename	**Description**
CONTROL.INI	Contains the various settings that you can access and modify through the Control Panel applets. These settings include desktop, printer, driver, and font settings. This file is discussed in more detail in Chapter 11, "Using the Control Panel."
PROGMAN.INI	Contains information that defines the position and contents of your program groups. This file is discussed in more detail in Chapter 9, "Using Program Manager."
SYSTEM.INI	Contains information that Windows needs to operate properly on your system. This file is discussed in detail in this chapter.
WIN.INI	Contains information that Windows uses to configure and set up the Windows environment. This file is discussed in detail in this chapter.
WINFILE.INI	Contains information that is used by File Manager. This file is discussed in detail in Chapter 10, "Using File Manager."

You'll find two basic types of initialization files on your system: Windows initialization files and private initialization files.

The Windows initialization files are files provided by Windows that include WIN.INI and SYSTEM.INI. Windows initialization files are used by Windows and Windows components. These files can also be used by other Windows applications to store information.

Private initialization files are created and used exclusively by one application. You will likely find dozens of private initialization files on your system. An application uses a private initialization file to store information that it needs to operate. When you remove an application, you can remove any private initialization files used by the application.

The two most important initialization files are the SYSTEM.INI files and WIN.INI files. We'll examine these files in detail in this chapter. But first, let's learn a little more about initialization files and how you can edit them.

Understanding Sections and Entries

All Windows initialization files are formatted in the same way. Each initialization file is made up of sections and entries. Each section in an initialization file is formatted as follows:

[section]

entry=value

where

[section] is the name of the section. The section name is always enclosed in brackets.

entry is the name of a line in the section

value is any value assigned to the entry

Sections may contain one or more entries. The various sections of an initialization file can appear in any order.

Although most initialization files do not contain comments, they can be added by preceding the entry with a semicolon. The semicolon must be the first character in the comment line.

Editing Initialization Files

Initialization files are simple text files and have the .INI file extension. The Windows initialization files are usually found in the WINDOWS directory and sometimes in the WINDOWS\SYSTEM directory. Private initialization files can be found in the WINDOWS directory, the WINDOWS\SYSTEM directory, or the application directory.

Initialization files are ASCII files and can be modified using any text editor including your word processor. Consider, however, using SysEdit or Notepad to edit your .INI files because these are simple text editors. Word processors such as Write, Word, and WordPerfect format text by default and add hidden characters in the text. You can damage your .INI files if you forget to save the file as ASCII text. Just to be safe, use either SysEdit or Notepad as outlined in the following sections.

Using SysEdit

SysEdit is loaded onto your system when Windows is installed. SysEdit is an undocumented feature of Windows, so you won't find an icon for SysEdit in Program Manager. To create an icon for SysEdit follow these steps:

1. Open the Accessories group window by double-clicking the Accessories group icon.

2. Choose File, New from the Program Manager menu bar. The New Program Object dialog box appears.

3. Make sure the Program Item button is selected and click OK. The Program Items Properties dialog box appears.

4. In the Description edit field, type **SysEdit**.

5. Click the Browse button and search the WINDOWS and WINDOWS\SYSTEM directories for the file SYSEDIT.EXE. Once you locate the file, highlight the filename and click OK. The path to the file appears in the Command Line edit field.

6. In the Working Directory edit field, type the path for your WINDOWS directory. For example, type **C:\WINDOWS**.

7. Click OK. The icon for SysEdit is displayed in the Accessories group.

To start SysEdit, double-click the SysEdit icon in the Accessories program group. SysEdit is shown in Figure 12.1. When SysEdit starts, it automatically opens document windows for AUTOEXEC.BAT, CONFIG.SYS, WIN.INI, and SYSTEM.INI. Depending on the version and configuration of your Windows environment, other document windows may be opened. To edit any of the open files, simply click on the window that contains the appropriate file and make any necessary changes.

Note

SysEdit can only be used to edit the files that are automatically opened when it starts. To edit private initialization files and other Windows initialization files, use Notepad.

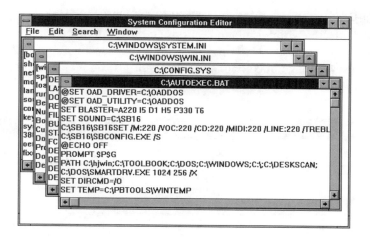

Fig. 12.1
Using SysEdit to edit initialization files.

Using Notepad

Notepad is a simple ASCII text editor. You can start Notepad by double-clicking the Notepad icon in the Accessories program group. Notepad is shown in Figure 12.2. With Notepad, you can open any .INI file from any directory. Once the appropriate .INI file has been opened, you can edit the file and save any changes. Notepad supports simple text-editing features such as cut and paste.

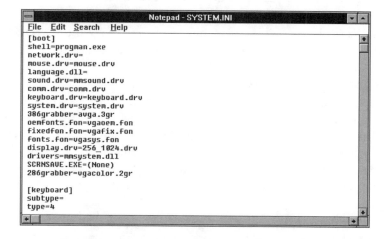

Fig. 12.2
Using Notepad to edit initialization files.

Understanding SYSTEM.INI

The SYSTEM.INI file is loaded when Windows is started. This file contains sections of entries that define system information needed by Windows to operate properly. You will need to understand the SYSTEM.INI sections and entries to effectively uninstall applications and to clean up your system. The SYSTEM.INI file typically contains the sections described in Table 12.2. Your SYSTEM.INI file may not contain all of these entries and may contain additional entries not listed in Table 12.2.

Table 12.2 Sections in the SYSTEM.INI File	
Section	**Description**
[386Enh]	Specifies information used by Windows in 386 enhanced mode
[boot]	Specifies drivers and Windows modules
[boot.description]	Specifies the names of the devices you can change using Windows Setup
[drivers]	Specifies the aliases assigned to installable driver files
[keyboard]	Specifies keyboard information
[mci]	Specifies Media Control Interface (MCI) drivers
[NonWindowsApp]	Specifies information used by DOS applications
[standard]	Specifies information used by Windows when running in standard mode

Let's take a look at some of the more important sections of the SYSTEM.INI file and the types of entries that you are most likely to find in these sections.

The [386Enh] Section

The [386Enh] section of the SYSTEM.INI file contains information that Windows uses for virtual-memory page swapping, virtual-memory drivers, and 32-bit disk access. The [386Enh] section contains the entries listed in Table 12.3; however, your SYSTEM.INI file may not contain all of these entries and may contain entries not listed here. You do not want to modify the majority of the entries in this section because modifying an entry can cause Windows to crash.

Table 12.3 The [386Enh] Section	
Entry	**Description**
32BitDiskAccess=<on or off>	Controls 32-bit disk access. When set to on, Windows attempts to use 32-bit access. Otherwise, Windows does not use 32-bit disk access. The default value is off.

Entry	Description
AllVMsExclusive=<True or False>	When True, forces all DOS windows to run in full-screen mode. The default value is False.
COMBoostTime=<milliseconds>	Specifies the maximum amount of time that a virtual machine is allowed to process a COM interrupt. The default value is 2.
COMMdrv30=<True or False>	When True, the virtual COM driver (VCD) uses its own copy of the interrupt handler for the serial communications driver resulting in improved performance. The default value is False.
COMxFIFO=<0 or 1>	Specifies the status of the FIFO buffer for the appropriate COM port's 16550 Universal Asynchronous Receiver Transmitter (UART). True enables the FIFO buffer. The default value is False.
COMIrqSharing=<True or False>	Indicates whether COM interrupt lines are shareable between multiple serial ports or with other devices. The default value is True for MicroChannel and EISA machines. It is False for all other machines.
DOSPromptExitInstruc=<True or False>	When enabled, a message is displayed providing exit and task-switching information whenever an MS-DOS prompt is started.
DualDisplay=<True or False>	Specifies whether a secondary display device is being used.
EMMExclude=<paragraph range>	Specifies a particular memory range that Windows will not scan when looking for unused address space.
EMMInclude=<paragraph range>	Specifies a particular memory range that Windows uses as unused space regardless of what is there.
EMMPageFrame=<paragraph>	Specifies the starting paragraph where the 64K page frame begins when Windows cannot find a suitable page frame. The default is none.
EMMSize=<kilobytes>	Specifies the amount of memory available for mapping as expanded memory. The default size is 65,536.
EnableSharingPopUps=<True or False>	Specifies whether a SHARE.EXE sharing-violation message is displayed when a sharing violation occurs when using VSHARE. The default value is False.
FileSysChange=<on or off>	Indicates whether file information in File Manager is updated when a DOS application creates, renames, or deletes a file. The default value is off.

(continues)

Table 12.3 Continued

Entry	Description
InDOSPolling=<Yes or No>	When enabled, prevents Windows from running other applications when memory-resident software has the InDOS flag set. The default is No.
INT28Critical=<True or False>	Indicates whether a critical section is needed to handle INT28h interrupts used by memory-resident software. The default value is True.
LocalReboot=<on or off>	Indicates whether the Ctrl+Alt+Del key combination can be used to quit applications that cause an unrecoverable error. The default value is on.
MaxBPs=<number>	Specifies the maximum number of breakpoints that the virtual memory manager can use. The default value is 200.
MaxCOMPort=<number>	Specifies the maximum number of COM ports supported. The default value is 4.
NetAsynchFallback=<True or False>	Indicates whether Windows attempts to save a failing NetBIOS request. The default value is False.
NetAsynchTimeout=<seconds>	Specifies the timeout period when Windows will enter a critical section to service a NetBIOS request. The default value is 5.
NetCard=<filenames>	Specifies one or more virtual device drivers for the network adapter.
NetDMASize=<kilobytes>	Specifies the DMA buffer size for NetBIOS transport software. The default value is 32 for MicroChannel machines or 0 for all other machines.
NetHeapSize=<kilobytes>	Specifies the size of the data-transfer buffers in conventional memory used to transfer data over a network. The default value is 12.
NetMisc=<filenames>	Specifies one or more virtual device drivers needed to run your network software.
Network=<filenames>	Specifies the virtual network drivers that Windows needs.
ReflectDosInt2A=<True or False>	Indicates whether Windows consumes or reflects DOS INT 2A signals. The default value is False.
SecondNet=<filename>	Specifies the virtual network drivers for additional networks installed during Setup.
SyncTime=<True or False>	Indicates whether Windows periodically adjusts its time with the computer's CMOS clock. The default value is True.

Entry	Description
TimerCriticalSection=< milliseconds>	Specifies the timeout period when Windows should go into a critical section. The default value is 0.
Transport=<filenames>	Specifies the network protocol virtual device driver file.
TrapTimerPorts=<True or False>	Indicates whether Windows traps read and write operations to the system timer ports. The default is True.
V86ModelLANAs= <number, number>	Specifies the LANA numbers for the real-mode protocols and NetBIOS recognized by Windows.
VirtualHDIrq=<on or off>	Indicates whether Windows can terminate interrupts from the hard drive controller. The default value is on for AT-compatible computers.

The [boot] Section

The [boot] section of the SYSTEM.INI file contains vital information needed for the proper operation of Windows. The values assigned to the entries in this section are determined by Windows during Setup. Table 12.4 lists the entries that you will typically find in the [boot] section.

Caution

Do not modify or delete the entries in the [boot] section of the SYSTEM.INI file. These entries are required for the proper operation of Windows.

Review the [boot] section of the SYSTEM.INI file before cleaning up your system. The [boot] section provides insight into what files are actually being used by your system. Never delete a file that is referenced in this section.

Table 12.4 The [boot] Section

Entry	Description
286grabber=<filename>	Specifies the grabber file Windows uses with 286 machines.
386grabber=<filename>	Specifies the grabber file Windows uses with 386 or greater machines.
comm.drv=<filename>	Specifies the name of the communications driver used by Windows.

(continues)

Table 12.4 Continued	
Entry	**Description**
display.drv=<filename>	Specifies the name of the driver file that Windows uses for the display adapter.
drivers=<filename>	Specifies the name of a driver or library file used by Windows.
fixedfon.fon=<filename>	Specifies the name of one of the font files used by Windows for screen displays.
fonts.fon=<filename>	Specifies the name of one of the font files used by Windows for screen displays.
keyboard.drv=<filename>	Specifies the name of the keyboard driver used by Windows.
language.dll=<filename>	Specifies the name of the language library Windows uses for international languages.
mouse.drv=<filename>	Specifies the name of the mouse driver used by Windows.
network.drv=<filename>	Specifies the name of the network driver used by Windows.
oemfonts.fon=<filename>	Specifies the name of one of the font files used by Windows for screen displays.
shell=<filename>	Specifies the application that is initiated when Windows is started. For most people, this file is winfile.exe, the Windows Program Manager.
sound.drv=<filename>	Specifies the name of the sound driver Windows uses for multimedia sound services.
system.drv=<filename>	Specifies the name of the system driver being used by Windows.

The [boot.description] Section

The [boot.description] section of the SYSTEM.INI file contains entries that associate descriptive text strings with the devices that you can modify with Windows Setup.

Caution

Do not modify the entries in the [boot.description] section of the SYSTEM.INI file. Changing these entries will prohibit you from being able to use Setup to update drivers and to modify system settings.

The [drivers] Section

The [drivers] section of the SYSTEM.INI file contains a list of names, or aliases, assigned to installable drivers. The entries in this section use the following format:

    alias=filename [parameters]

where

    alias is the alias name of the installable driver

    filename is the name of the driver file

    parameters defines optional parameters for the installable driver

Entries in this section may be associated with entries in the [boot] section of the SYSTEM.INI file. If a driver includes parameters, you must assign an alias to the driver in the [drivers] section and specify the driver by alias name in the [boot] section. Table 12.5 lists the drivers that support the Windows multimedia capabilities. These files are often assigned aliases in the [drivers] section of the SYSTEM.INI file.

Table 12.5   Multimedia Driver Files

Filename	Description
MCICDA.DRV	MCI CD-audio driver
MCISEQ.DRV	MCI MIDI driver
MCIWAVE.DRV	MCI waveform audio driver
MIDIMAP.DRV	MIDI mapper driver
MMSOUND.DRV	Multimedia sound driver
MPU401.DRV	MIDI driver for MPU401 compatibles
MSADLIB.DRV	MIDI driver for Adlib compatibles
SNDBLST.DRV	Sound Blaster 1.5 DSP driver
SNDBLST2.DRV	Sound Blaster 2.0 DSP driver
TIMER.DRV	Multimedia timer driver

The [keyboard] Section

The [keyboard] section of the SYSTEM.INI file contains specific information about the system keyboard. The entries in this section are created and values are assigned during Windows Setup.

Caution

Do not modify the settings of the [keyboard] section of the SYSTEM.INI file. These settings are required for the proper operation of the keyboard.

The [mci] Section

The [mci] section of the SYSTEM.INI file lists Media Control Interface (MCI) device drivers. The settings found in the [mci] section are typically modified from the Control Panel Drivers applet. Table 12.6 lists the entries typically found in the [mci] section.

Table 12.6   The [mci] Section

Entry	Description
AVIVideo=<filename>	Specifies the filename of the MCI device driver used to play back AVI video clips. The default setting is mciavi.drv.
CDAudio=<filename>	Specifies the filename of the MCI driver used to control audio CD players. The default driver is MDICDA.DRV.
Sequencer=<filename>	Specifies the filename of the MCI driver used to control MIDI sequencers. The default driver is MCISEQ.DRV.
Videodisc=<filename> [com port]	Specifies the filename of the MCI driver used to control external videodisc players. The default setting is MCIPIONR.DRV COM1.
WaveAudio=<filename> [buffer size]	Specifies the filename of the MCI driver used to control the recording and playback of waveform audio files. The default setting is MCIWAVE.DRV 4.

The [NonWindowsApp] Section

The [NonWindowsApp] section of the SYSTEM.INI file contains entries that control the performance of DOS applications running under Windows. Table 12.7 lists the entries that are often found in the [NonWindowsApp] section.

Table 12.7 The [NonWindowsApp] Section	
Entry	**Description**
CommandEnvSize=<bytes>	Specifies the size of the COMMAND.COM environment for MS-DOS prompts and batch files under Windows. The default value is 0.
DisablePositionSave=<0 or 1>	Disables the saving positions and fonts for a DOS application in the DOSAPP.INI file when the application is closed. The default value is 0.
FontChangeEnable=<0 or 1>	Indicates whether the font can be changed when running DOS applications in a window.
LocalTSRs=<list>	Lists the TSRs that are compatible with individual virtual machines. The default is DOSEDIT, CED.
MouseInDosBox=<0 or 1>	Indicates whether you want mouse support with your DOS applications running under Windows.
ScrollFrequency=<number>	Indicates the number of lines to scroll a DOS application running in a window before the window area is updated.

Understanding WIN.INI

The WIN.INI file is loaded by Windows during startup. The WIN.INI file contains settings that control the Windows environment. These settings provide information about printers, fonts, ports, and screen colors. Pay close attention to the various sections and entries in the WIN.INI file. These sections and entries provide detailed information that you need to know during uninstall and cleanup sessions. The WIN.INI file typically contains the sections described in Table 12.8; however, your WIN.INI file may not contain all of these entries and may contain additional entries not listed in Table 12.8.

Table 12.8 Sections in the WIN.INI File	
Section	**Description**
[colors]	Specifies the colors used for the Windows display.
[desktop]	Specifies the appearance of the desktop and the position of icons and windows.
[devices]	Lists the active output devices that provide backwards compatibility with Windows applications designed for earlier versions of Windows.

(continues)

Table 12.8 Continued	
Section	**Description**
[embedding]	Defines the server objects used in object linking and embedding (OLE).
[extensions]	Specifies the file extensions that are to be associated with a particular application.
[fonts]	Lists the screen font files loaded by Windows.
[fontSubstitutes]	Lists font pairs that Windows treats as interchangeable.
[intl]	Describes how items for international countries are displayed.
[mci extensions]	Specifies the file extensions that are to be associated with the Media Control Interface (MCI) devices.
[network]	Describes network connections and settings.
[ports]	Lists the available ports.
[printerPorts]	Lists the active and inactive output devices that can be accessed by Windows.
[programs]	Lists any additional paths that Windows will search when attempting to find the application associated with a data file.
[sound]	Lists the sound files associated with each system event.
[TrueType]	Describes options for using TrueType fonts.
[Windows]	Describes various visual aspects of the Windows environment.
[Windows Help]	Defines various settings used for the Windows Help window and dialog boxes.

Let's take a closer look at some of the more important sections and the types of entries that you are most likely to find in these sections.

The [colors] Section

The [colors] section of the WIN.INI file defines the colors that Windows uses to paint the various components of the Windows display. The [colors] section contains entries in the following format:

    component=red green blue

Table 12.9 lists the various components for which Windows assigns colors. Each component has a red, green, and blue (RGB) value associated with it. The RGB value defines the mixture of red, green, and blue that Windows uses to render the color on the screen. The red, green, and blue values range from 0 to 255 inclusive. For example, an RGB value of 0, 0, 255 indicates true blue.

Table 12.9 Windows Components for the [colors] Section	
Component	**Description**
ActiveBorder	Specifies the border of the active window.
ActiveTitle	Specifies the title bar of the active window.
AppWorkspace	Specifies the application workspace for Windows applications.
Background	Specifies the desktop.
ButtonFace	Specifies the face of the dialog box and toolbar buttons.
ButtonShadow	Specifies the button shadow used to give the buttons a 3-D look.
ButtonText	Specifies the button text.
GrayText	Specifies dimmed text indicating unavailability.
Hilight	Specifies the background of highlighted text.
HilightText	Specifies highlighted text.
InactiveBorder	Specifies the border of an inactive window.
InactiveTitle	Specifies the title bar of an inactive window.
InactiveTitleText	Specifies the text in an inactive window.
Menu	Specifies the menu background.
MenuText	Specifies the text for menu items.
ScrollBar	Specifies the scroll bars.
TitleText	Specifies the title bar text.
Window	Specifies the window workspace.
WindowFrame	Specifies the window border.
WindowText	Specifies the text within a window.

The [desktop] Section

The [desktop] section contains settings that control the appearance of the Windows background, called the desktop. This section also controls the positioning of windows and program icons. The majority of the entries in this section can be modified through the Control Panel. Table 12.10 lists the entries typically found in the [desktop] section.

Table 12.10 Entries in the [desktop] Section	
Entry	**Description**
GridGranularity=<pixels>	Indicates whether Windows aligns application windows using an invisible grid. This value ranges between 0 to 49 inclusive and determines the spacing between grid lines. The default value is 0.
IconSpacing=<pixels>	Specifies the number of pixels that Windows places horizontally between icons. The default value is 77.
IconTitleFaceName=<fontname>	Specifies the name of the font to be used to display icon titles. The default font is MS SansSerif.
IconTitleSize=<fontsize>	Specifies the font size Windows uses to display icon titles. The default value is 8.
IconTitleWrap=<0 to 1>	Indicates whether icon titles are allowed to wrap to more than one line. The default value of 1 enables icon title wrapping. Windows automatically increases the icon vertical spacing when title wrapping is enabled.
IconVerticalSpacing=<pixels>	Specifies the number of pixels that Windows places vertically between icons. The default value is 77.
Pattern=<value1 to value8>	Specifies eight values for the eight by eight pixel bitmap that Windows uses to paint the screen background. Each of the eight values is the decimal equivalent to the binary value that describes one line in the bitmap. No pattern is defined by default.
TileWallpaper=<0 or 1>	Indicates whether the Windows wallpaper is tiled or centered. The default value of 0 indicates the wallpaper centered on the screen. A value of 1 indicates the is wallpaper is tiled.
Wallpaper=<filename>	Specifies the filename of the bitmap image used for the Windows wallpaper. No wallpaper is defined by default.

The [fonts] Section

The [fonts] section of the WIN.INI file describes the font files that Windows loads when Windows is started. The entries in this section use the following format:

fontname=fontfile

where

fontname is the typeface of the font

fontfile is the name of the font file and includes a file extension (usually .FON or .FOT)

By reviewing this section, you can determine which font files are associated with each font typeface.

The [mci extensions] Section

The [mci extensions] section of the WIN.INI file contains settings that associate a type of media file with a particular Media Control Interface (MCI) device driver. The entries in the [mci extensions] section are formatted as follows:

extension=mcidevice

where

extension is the extension for a media file such as .WAV, .AVI, .FLC, or .MID

mcidevice is the mci device such as wave audio, sequencer, animation, or video

The [printerPorts] Section

The [printerPorts] section lists the active and inactive output devices (printers, plotters, and so forth) that can be accessed by Windows. The entries in this section have the following format:

printername=drivername,port,timeout1,timeout2

where

printername is a line of description text such as HP LaserJet IIP

drivername is the name of the printer's driver file such as HPPCL—no file extension is specified but the .DRV file extension can be assumed

port is the port where the printer is connected such as LPT1:

timeout1 is the Device Not Selected timeout period in seconds

timeout2 is the Transmission Retry timeout period in seconds

This section is very useful when you are trying to delete printer driver files. By looking at the printer name and printer driver, you can determine which printer driver file is associated with which printer.

The [Windows] Section

The entries in the [Windows] section of the WIN.INI file control various aspects of the operation of Windows. The [Windows] section often contains the entries listed in Table 12.11. Your WIN.INI file may or may not contain all of the entries listed here.

Table 12.11   Entries in the [Windows] Section

Entry	Description
Beep=<yes or no>	Indicates whether Windows sounds a warning beep when you attempt an action that is not permitted or supported.
BorderWidth=<pixels>	Specifies the number of pixels Windows uses for the sizable borders of application windows. The default size is 3. This value can range from 1 to 49, inclusive.
CoolSwitch=<0 or 1>	Indicates whether Windows enables fast task switching. Fast task switching allows you to use the Alt+Tab key sequence to switch between applications.
CursorBlinkRate=<milliseconds>	Specifies the amount of time between each blink of the cursor. The default value is 530.
Documents=<extensions>	Specifies the file extensions that Windows acknowledges as documents. The file extensions listed in this section are not listed in the [extensions] section of WIN.INI.
DoubleClickHeight=<pixels>	Specifies the maximum vertical amount (in pixels) that the mouse can move between clicks for the input to be considered a double-click.
DoubleClickWidth=<pixels>	Specifies the maximum horizontal amount (in pixels) that the mouse can move between clicks for the input to be considered a double-click.
Load=<filename(s)>	Specifies one or more applications that are to be launched and minimized when Windows is started. If you delete a file referenced in this section, Windows will give you an error message during startup.
MenuDropAlignment=<0 or 1>	Indicates whether menus are right-aligned or left-aligned with the menu title when they are opened. 0 indicates menus are left-aligned; 1 indicates menus are right-aligned.
MenuShowDelay=<milliseconds>	Defines the amount of time Windows waits before displaying a cascading menu. This value is 0 for 386 and higher machines and 400 for 286 machines.

Entry	Description
Programs=<extensions>	Indicates the types of files that Windows considers application files. The default file extensions that Windows recognizes as application files are .EXE, .COM, .BAT, and .PIF.
Run=<filename(s)>	Specifies one or more applications that are to be launched when Windows is started. If you delete a file referenced in this section, Windows will give you an error message during startup. Adding or deleting a program item from the Windows Startup group does not alter this entry.
ScreenSaveActive= <0 or 1>	Indicates whether Windows displays a screensaver using the built-in Desktop screensaver feature. 0 indicates no screensaver is to be displayed.
ScreenSaveTimeout= <seconds>	Specifies the amount of time the system must be idle before Windows will start the built-in Desktop screensaver.

The [Windows Help] Section

The [Windows Help] section contains settings that specify the size and position of the Help window and dialog boxes. You can also specify the color of text displayed within the Help window. Table 12.12 lists the entries that you typically find in the [Windows Help] section.

Table 12.12   Entries in the [Windows Help] Section

Entry	Description
IFJumpColor=<red, green, blue>	Specifies the color (using red-green-blue (RGB) values) of text that, when selected by the user, leads to a new Help window using a different Help file.
IFPopupColor=<red, green, blue>	Specifies the color (using red-green-blue (RGB) values) of text that, when selected by the user, displays a popup window located in a different Help file.
JumpColor=<red, green, blue>	Specifies the color (using red-green-blue (RGB) values) of text that, when selected by the user, opens a new window of Help information.
MacroColor=<red, green, blue>	Specifies the color (using red-green-blue (RGB) values) of text that, when selected by the user, runs a Help macro.
PopupColor=<red, green, blue>	Specifies the color (using red-green-blue (RGB) values) of text that, when selected by the user, opens a popup window.

From Here...

Initialization files contain configuration information and settings for Windows and Windows applications. Now that you are familiar with initialization files, you are ready to review a sample uninstall session.

- Chapter 13, "Uninstalling Microsoft Office: A Sample Uninstall Session," takes you step-by-step through a complete uninstall session.

- Chapter 14, "Learning about UnInstaller 3.0," introduces you to UnInstaller 3.0 and its many features.

Chapter 13

Uninstalling Microsoft Office: A Sample Uninstall Session

Now that you have learned the uninstall process and how to use Program Manager, File Manager, and the Control Panel, let's go through an example uninstall session using the steps covered in Chapter 4, "Learning the Unintall Process."

In this chapter, you learn to

- Review an uninstall session

- Learn what uninstall steps can be skipped and why

- See how you can modify the uninstall process to meet your needs

Reviewing the Example

In this chapter, you'll go through an entire example uninstall session. This chapter outlines the steps that I went through to remove Microsoft Office with Windows for Workgroups from my system. As you may know, Microsoft Office contains several applications, including Microsoft Word, Excel, PowerPoint, and Access. I installed Microsoft Office from a CD-ROM onto my D drive. (I have two hard drives in my system.) Windows is on my C drive. I did a full installation from the CD-ROM with the exception of documentation files which I access from the CD-ROM.

So that you can understand what I did, I followed all the steps outlined in Chapters 5, 6, 7, and 8. I did not use every substep for each of the four steps in the process. However, I did explain why I skipped certain substeps.

Step 1: Preparing Your System

As you learned back in Chapter 5, "Step 1: Preparing Your System," you need to do a little bit of preparation before you start removing application files. The process that was outlined in that chapter involved the following substeps:

- Getting System Information

- Creating the BOOTLOG.TXT File

- Reviewing the Windows Files

- Moving and Organizing Files and Directories

- Backing Up the System

I followed these substeps when I was preparing to uninstall Microsoft Office from my computer. Take a look at how I performed each of these substeps.

Getting System Information

In Chapter 5, you learned several ways to get the information you need to uninstall applications. These include the following:

- Reviewing the Initialization Files

- Reviewing Fonts

- Reviewing File Associations

- Reviewing Drivers

- Getting Information from the Program Group and Items

- Getting a File List of the Application Setup Disks

First, I need to know as much about my system as possible. From what I know and what I can determine from my system manual, a description of my system follows:

CPU: 486 DX2/50

Display Adapter: Cirrius

Display Adapter Mode: 640 by 480, 256 Colors

Mouse: Microsoft Serial

Keyboard: Enhanced 101-Key US

Memory: 16 MB

Floppy Drive: 3.5" 1.44 MB

Hard Drives: 340 MB Drive C and 540 MB Drive D

Removable Drive: IOMEGA Bernoulli Transportable

CD-ROM: Creative Labs drive

Sound Card: Sound Blaster

Video Capture Card: Video Blaster

Scanner: HP IIC Color Scanner and Adapter

Printers: HP LaserJet IIP and CalComp ColorMaster Plus 6603PS

Tape Backup: Conner 250MQ Parallel Port

After I jot down the system information that I need, I review my initialization files and print out copies of my WIN.INI and SYSTEM.INI files. I use the Notepad application to open, review, and print copies of these files.

Next, I go to the Control Panel and review my list of fonts using the Fonts applet and find several fonts that I never use and want to delete. I make a note of these fonts to remove later in the process. The fonts that I want to delete include the Freeport and Kids fonts installed by CorelDRAW!. Although these are not fonts installed by Microsoft Office, I want to clean up my system as I uninstall Microsoft Office.

The next step in the process involves determining the file associations used by the applications in Microsoft Office. By reviewing the [extensions] section of WIN.INI, I am able to find the following entries that are used with Microsoft Office.

doc=D:\MSOFFICE\WINWORD\WINWORD.EXE ^.doc

dot=D:\MSOFFICE\WINWORD\WINWORD.EXE ^.dot

rtf=D:\MSOFFICE\WINWORD\WINWORD.EXE ^.rtf

mdb=D:\MSOFFICE\ACCESS\MSACCESS.EXE ^.MDB

xla=D:\MSOFFICE\EXCEL\excel.exe ^.xla

xlc=D:\MSOFFICE\EXCEL\excel.exe ^.xlc

xll=D:\MSOFFICE\EXCEL\excel.exe ^.xll

xlm=D:\MSOFFICE\EXCEL\excel.exe ^.xlm

xls=D:\MSOFFICE\EXCEL\excel.exe ^.xls

xlt=D:\MSOFFICE\EXCEL\excel.exe ^.xlt

xlw=D:\MSOFFICE\EXCEL\excel.exe ^.xlw

ppt=D:\MSOFFICE\POWERPNT\POWERPNT.EXE ^.ppt

From these entries, I determine the following:

- Microsoft Word for Windows uses the following file associations: .DOC, .DOT, and .RTF.

- Microsoft Access uses the following file association: .MDB.

- Microsoft Excel uses the the following files associations: .XLA, .XLC, .XLL, .XLM, .XLS, .XLT, and .XLW.

- Microsoft PowerPoint uses the following file association: .PPT.

Once I determine the file associations for the Microsoft Office applications, I use the Control Panel Drivers applet to review my list of drivers. After reviewing my list of multimedia drivers, I determine that none of these drivers needs to be removed. This makes sense because I'm not modifying any of the multimedia components on my system.

Next, I go to the Microsoft Office program group to review the program items in the group. By reviewing the properties of each program item in the group, I am able to determine the information listed in Table 13.1.

Table 13.1 Information from Program Items

Program Item	Path	Item File
Word	D:\MSOFFICE\WINWORD	WINWORD.EXE
Excel	D:\MSOFFICE\EXCEL	EXCEL.EXE
PowerPoint	D:\MSOFFICE\POWERPNT	POWERPNT.EXE
Graph Auto Convert	C:\WINDOWS\MSAPPS\MSGRAPH5	AUTOCONV.EXE
Office Readme Help	D:\MSOFFICE	OFREADME.HLP
Online Documentation	Path to CD-ROM drive	None
MS Office	D:\MSOFFICE	MSOFFICE.EXE
Access	D:\MSOFFICE\ACCESS	MSACCESS.EXE

Program Item	Path	Item File
Access Workgroup Administrator	D:\MSOFFICE\ACCESS	WRKGADM.EXE

From the information listed in Table 13.1, I can tell that most of the application files are located in a subdirectory of the MSOFFICE directory on my D hard drive. The Graph Auto Convert files are located in the MSAPPS subdirectory under my WINDOWS directory. The online documentation is not installed on my hard drive because the path referenced my CD-ROM drive.

The last thing I need to do in this substep is to review my setup disk and to create a list of application files from the setup disk (in this case CD-ROM). After reviewing the files on the CD-ROM drive, I decide that it is not reasonable to do this in this case because of the number of files involved. The MS Office CD-ROM contains dozens of directories and approximately 500 files. An exhaustive search for this many files is unreasonable. However, if I were only removing one part of Microsoft Office, I would print a list of files for the one application. A single MS Office application would only involve a few directories and few dozen files. In this case, a search of each application file is reasonable and doesn't require much time.

Creating the BOOTLOG.TXT File

Creating the BOOTLOG.TXT file is easy. I exit and then restart Windows with the C:\WINDOWS /B command line. Once Windows starts, I open File Manager and change the name of BOOTLOG.TXT to BOOTLOG1.TXT.

Reviewing the Windows Files

I skipped this step because I am very familiar with Windows and its file structure. If you are not familiar with Windows files, review the "Reviewing the Windows Files" section in Chapter 5.

Moving and Organizing Files and Directories

In this step, I review all the files in the subdirectories found in the MSOFFICE directory on my D drive. My goal here is to locate, review, and move any of the document files that I created and want to save. Using File Manager, I move those document files that I want to save to a new directory called OFFDOCS (for Office Documents). While reviewing the files in the MSOFFICE subdirectories, I notice that almost all of the files are dated 3/31/94. I jot this date down to use when searching for stray application files.

Backing Up the System

At this point, I am ready to back up my system. I decide to perform two levels of backup. The first level is to copy my initialization files—WIN.INI, SYSTEM.INI, AUTOEXEC.BAT, CONFIG.SYS, Windows group (.GRP) files—to a floppy disk.

The second level is to completely back up both my hard drives. I use my tape backup unit to back up all my data. This takes several hours and several tapes because I am backing up two drives and about 1 gigabyte of disk space. If you have a 200 MB hard drive, you should be able to back up your system in about an hour.

Step 2: Removing Application Files

This step is easy but scary. It is easy because of the preparation from Step 1. It's scary because I am deleting many files from my system. Let's look at the substeps that I perform to remove the Microsoft Office application files. As you recall from Chapter 6, "Step 2: Removing Application Files," the three substeps in this step are:

- Deleting Program Items and Groups

- Deleting the Application Directory

- Removing Other Application Files

Let's take a closer look at how to perform each of these substeps.

Deleting Program Items and Groups

This step is really simple: all I have to do is go to Program Manager, select the Microsoft Office program group icon, and press the Del key. After confirming the delete operation, I am done. Program Manager removes the program group, all program items in the group, and the .GRP file associated with the group.

Note

By default, Microsoft Office usually places a copy of the Microsoft Office icon in the StartUp group; however, I removed the Office program item from the StartUp group long ago and don't have to remove it in this step.

Deleting the Application Directory

Next I need to delete the application directory. Back in Step 1, I moved all the files that I wanted to save to a new directory. I also learned that almost all my files were in the D:\MSOFFICE directory or one of its subdirectories. Therefore, all I need to do is to go to File Manager, select the MSOFFICE directory icon from the left side of the directory window, and press Del.

After confirming that I want to delete all the files, File Manager deletes the directory and all of its files and subdirectories. In Step 1, I also learned that some of the application files were in the MSAPPS directory under WINDOWS. I review that directory and learn that this directory contains several subdirectories used by Microsoft Office. I remove the MSAPPS directory as well.

Removing Other Application Files

The last step is to delete any stray application files. As you may recall from Chapter 6, "Step 2: Removing Application Files," several tricks can be used to locate stray application files including:

- Using file dates
- Using filenames
- Using file types
- Using file properties

To begin with, I search for files with the file date 3/31/94. As you recall, I noticed this date was used by most of the application files in the MSOFFICE directory. I search the WINDOWS and WINDOWS/SYSTEM directories.

In the WINDOWS directory, I find four files with this file date. Three of the files are .INI files that I am able to identify and delete. The fourth file is a .DLL file. Because .DLL files can be shared by more than one application, I don't feel comfortable deleting the file and decide to leave it alone. After all, it's better to be safe than sorry.

In the WINDOWS/SYSTEM directory, I find almost 6 MB of files with this file date. Most of the files are .DLLs and font files. Of the 4 MB of .DLL files, I am able to delete about half with confidence. I select each .DLL file and review the properties using the Properties dialog box from File Manager, which I open by choosing File, Properties. In the Description field, I am able to determine the application that uses the file. I only delete files that contain descriptive text referring to MS Office: Word, PowerPoint, Excel, Access, or any of their subcomponents.

Searching for filenames is another trick that is often used to locate application files. Due to the large number of files involved in this uninstall, I don't search by filename.

The last trick I use is to search by file type. I search the WINDOWS and WINDOWS\SYSTEM directories for private .INI files. I find and delete all the private .INI files associated with Microsoft Office. I can tell by the filenames and contents which .INI files are associated with MS Office. For example, any private .INI file that contains any text form for Excel, PowerPoint, Access, or Word can be deleted. Also, private .INI files usually have a filename that is similar to the name of the application.

Step 3: Editing Initialization Files

Editing your .INI files is a task that requires special care. In this uninstall process, I perform the following substeps:

- Reviewing and Modifying SYSTEM.INI
- Reviewing and Modifying WIN.INI
- Reviewing CONFIG.SYS
- Reviewing AUTOEXEC.BAT

To perform these steps, I use SysEdit to open, review, and edit these files.

Reviewing and Modifying SYSTEM.INI

Using SysEdit, I review the SYSTEM.INI file for any reference to the MSOFFICE subdirectory or any of the applications in Microsoft Office. I am not able to find any reference that needs to be deleted.

Reviewing and Modifying WIN.INI

Again, I use SysEdit to review WIN.INI. I am looking for any reference to Microsoft Office and its applications. I find many references that need to be changed.

The first section that needs modification is the [extensions] section. This section associates file extensions with applications. I find several entries that make reference to Microsoft Office applications and the MSOFFICE directory. These entries are in the form of

```
xlt=D:\MSOFFICE\EXCEL\excel.exe ^.xlt
```

I delete all the entries containing a path that includes MSOFFICE.

The next section that needs modifying is the [embedding] section. I delete all the entries that contain any descriptive text of MS Office applications (Word, Excel, PowerPoint, Access) or any reference to the MSOFFICE directory.

Next, I find a section called [MSAPPS] that contains entries for the utilities in MSAPPS directory. Because I deleted this directory in the previous step, I remove the MSAPPS section.

As I review WIN.INI, I find several other sections that are added by Microsoft Office and used only by Office applications. The following sections can be removed:

- [Microsoft System Info]
- [MS Proofing Tools]
- [MS Graphic Import Filters]
- [MS Text Converters]
- [MS Setup (ACME) Table Files]
- [MS Word Text Converters]
- [MS Spreadsheet Converters]
- [MS Graphic Export Filters]

Once I remove all the appropriate entries and sections, I save WIN.INI.

Reviewing CONFIG.SYS

I review CONFIG.SYS and find nothing that needs to be changed. Unless an application is used exclusively with a particular hardware device (for example scanner software for use with a particular scanner) you will usually not have to modify the CONFIG.SYS file. MS Office is not associated with any of my hardware and did not modify my CONFIG.SYS file during installation.

Reviewing AUTOEXEC.BAT

I also review AUTOEXEC.BAT and find nothing to modify. Usually, Windows applications do not modify AUTOEXEC.BAT. If a Windows application does modify AUTOEXEC.BAT, it usually just adds the application directory to the PATH statement. MS Office did not modify my AUTOEXEC.BAT file during installation.

Step 4: Cleaning Up

By this time, I know that the worst is over. However, I still have a few items to clean up. As outlined in Chapter 8, "Step 4: Cleaning Up," the cleanup stage has the following substeps:

- Removing Unused, Unnecessary, and Outdated Files
- Removing Unwanted Windows Components Using Setup
- Removing Temporary Files
- Defragging the Hard Drive

Removing Unused, Unnecessary, and Outdated Files

The process of removing unused, unnecessary, and outdated files can be a lengthy process including any or all of the following:

- Deleting Private Initialization Files
- Removing Drivers and Driver Files
- Removing Printers and Printer Driver Files
- Removing Fonts and Font Files
- Removing Old Document Files
- Deleting .DLL Files
- Removing Duplicate Files

In my case, the process is quick and fairly painless because I only need to review a few files and delete a few fonts.

To begin with, I go to the WINDOWS directory to review the .INI files and find no .INI files that can be deleted.

The next thing I need to do is to remove the Freeport and Kids fonts using the Control Panel Fonts applet. With the Fonts applet, I select these fonts and remove them from the Windows list of installed fonts. I opt to allow the Fonts applet to remove the associated font files by selecting the Delete Font Files From Disk check box in the Remove Fonts dialog box.

> **Note**
>
> If you are running low on hard disk space or Windows system resources, spend more time on this step to make sure that you remove every possible file, font, and driver. Review Chapter 8, "Step 4: Cleaning Up," for more information on removing unnecessary files from your system.

Removing Unwanted Windows Components with Setup

I skipped this step because I don't need to remove any of the Windows Components. However, if you want to remove Windows applications and utilities that you don't use, you can use Windows Setup to remove components like CardFile, Backup, and Solitaire.

Removing Temporary Files

At this point, I exit Windows. At the DOS prompt, I go to my TEMP directory (as defined in AUTOEXEC.BAT) and delete all the temporary files. I then go to the WINDOWS directory and delete all the .TMP files. I find a few files in each of these directories but nothing really significant (in other words, the files aren't taking up much hard disk space).

Defragging the Hard Drive

The last thing I need to do is to defragment my hard drive. I use the DOS defragment utility which performs its job in only a few minutes. See Chapter 8, "Step 4: Cleaning Up," for information about defragging your hard drive.

Testing the System

It is now time to restart my system and test everything. I have no problems during the startup of my system or Windows, and when I test my applications, everything works.

Overall, the process only takes about an hour (with the exception of the system backup). During this uninstall process, I chose caution over efficiency. If I had a doubt about any file, I left it alone. By doing this, I left some files on my system that could have been deleted, but I am much less likely to cause problems this way.

From Here...

Now that you know how to uninstall applications, you are ready to learn how to use UnInstaller.

■ Chapter 14, "Learning about UnInstaller 3.0," introduces you to UnInstaller and its many features.

■ Chapter 15, "UnInstalling Applications with UnInstaller 3.0," teaches you how to use UnInstaller to uninstall applications and to clean up your system.

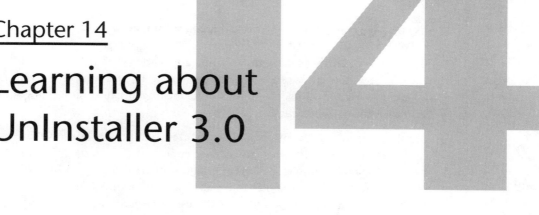

Chapter 14

Learning about UnInstaller 3.0

MicroHelp's UnInstaller 3.0 is a Windows utility that uninstalls applications. UnInstaller uses proprietary technology to intelligently search your hard drive and remove all files associated with an application.

In this chapter, you learn

- About UnInstaller 3.0 and SmartLinks
- To use the UnInstaller 3.0 interface
- To recognize the UnInstaller 3.0 features

Reviewing UnInstaller 3.0

MicroHelp defined the uninstaller utility market when UnInstaller was first released in 1992. Since then, UnInstaller has been the leader in the uninstaller utility market. UnInstaller 3.0, released in April of 1995, provides features that go way beyond the original concept of removing applications and their related files. UnInstaller 3.0 provides features for moving and archiving applications, cleaning up your files, editing your initialization files, and more. In this chapter we'll look at UnInstaller 3.0 and its many features.

Why UnInstaller?

UnInstaller is a utility that helps you uninstall applications and more. You have learned so far that Windows provides the basic components that you need to remove Windows applications and configure your system. So, why do you need UnInstaller to help you remove applications from your system?

As you have seen so far, removing an application takes a lot of work and you have to use several Windows components to properly perform the job. Utilities such as UnInstaller make uninstalling applications easier for you. With UnInstaller, a few clicks of the mouse can effectively, and completely, remove an application and all its related files while making any necessary changes to Windows initialization files.

Another reason that UnInstaller 3.0 is useful is that it offers features that can't be found in Windows or any of its components. In short, UnInstaller handles the most complex actions automatically. In addition, UnInstaller offers features that allow you to move applications, archive applications, remove duplicate files, locate orphaned files, edit initialization files, and much more.

SmartLinks

Perhaps the most significant feature of UnInstaller is its SmartLinks technology. UnInstaller uses SmartLinks to scan all the files on your system and determine the interrelationships between the files. By using SmartLinks technology, UnInstaller is able to determine which files are associated with each application. By determining this information, UnInstaller is able to effectively remove all the files associated with an application—no matter where the files are located, inside or outside of the application directory.

> **Note**
>
> When you first start UnInstaller, it builds a SmartLinks database. Whenever you select an option that requires the use of the SmartLinks database, UnInstaller asks you whether or not you want to update the database. Be sure to always update the database so that UnInstaller can make its decisions using the most up-to-date information.

The UnInstaller Window

The UnInstaller Application window, as shown in Figure 14.1 allows you to access all the UnInstaller features. The main components of the UnInstaller application window include the menu, the toolbar, and the status bar. Let's look more closely at the UnInstaller menu and the toolbar.

UnInstaller Menus

UnInstaller offers four menus in its menu bar: File, UnInstall, Cleanup, and Help. These menus allow you to invoke the UnInstaller commands and features. Table 14.1 lists the menu items available from the UnInstaller menu.

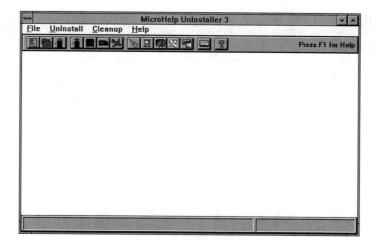

Fig. 14.1
The UnInstaller
Application
window.

Table 14.1   UnInstaller Menu Items

Menu Item	Description
File Menu	
View Report File	Displays reports created by UnInstaller or allows you to view the contents or information about a file
Preferences, Reports	Defines preferences for UnInstaller reports
Preferences, Backup	Defines preferences for backup options available for some UnInstaller features
Preferences, View	Defines user interface options for UnInstaller
Set/Change Password	Enables password security for UnInstaller
Restore	Opens UnInstaller's Restore feature for restoring deleted or archived applications
Exit	Exits UnInstaller
Uninstall Menu	
Delete Applications	Opens UnInstaller's Delete Applications feature for deleting applications
Archive Applications	Opens UnInstaller's Archive Applications feature for archiving applications
Move Applications	Opens UnInstaller's Move Applications feature for moving applications

(continues)

Table 14.1 Continued	
Menu Item	**Description**
File Menu	
Transport Applications	Opens UnInstaller's Transport Applications feature for transporting applications
Restore Archive	Opens UnInstaller's Restore feature and prepares it for restoring archive applications and files
Activate Transport	Opens UnInstaller's Restore feature and prepares it for restoring an application prepared for transport
Cleanup Menu	
Windows Cleanup	Opens UnInstaller's Windows Cleanup feature for locating and removing unnecessary files
INIClean	Opens UnInstaller's INIClean feature for viewing and editing initialization files
Duplicate File Finder	Opens UnInstaller's Duplicate File Finder feature for locating and deleting duplicate files
Orphan Finder	Opens UnInstaller's Orphan Finder feature for locating and removing orphaned files
Disk Data	Opens UnInstaller's Disk Data feature for viewing the directories and files on a hard drive
Help Menu	
Contents	Displays the contents of the UnInstaller Help file
Search for Help On	Displays a search window for the UnInstaller Help file
Technical Support	Displays information about MicroHelp technical support
How to Use Help	Provides information about using the Windows Help system
About	Displays UnInstaller version information

The UnInstaller Toolbar

UnInstaller provides a toolbar containing buttons that allow you to quickly access various UnInstaller features. Table 14.2 lists the icons used on the toolbar along with associated features.

Table 14.2 The UnInstaller Toolbar		
Icon	**Feature**	**Description**
	View Report File	Displays the View Report window
	Preferences	Displays the Preferences window
	Restore	Displays the Restore window
	Delete Applications	Displays the Delete Applications window
	Archive Applications	Displays the Archive Applications window
	Move Applications	Displays the Move Applications window
	Transport Applications	Displays the Transport Applications window
	Windows Cleanup	Displays the Windows Cleanup window
	INIClean	Displays the INIClean window
	Duplicate File Finder	Displays the Duplicate File Finder window
	Orphan Finder	Displays the Orphan Finder window
	Disk Data	Displays the Disk Data window
	Exit	Exits UnInstaller
	Help	Displays the UnInstaller Help window

UnInstaller Preferences

Whenever UnInstaller performs an action, it does so based on the information specified in Preferences window. The Preferences window provides configuration options that control the behavior of UnInstaller and its features. UnInstaller allows you to set the following preferences: Reports, Backup, and View. To access the UnInstaller Preferences window, click the Preferences button from the UnInstaller toolbar or select File, Preferences from the UnInstaller menu. The Preferences window is displayed in Figure 14.2.

Fig. 14.2
The Preferences
window.

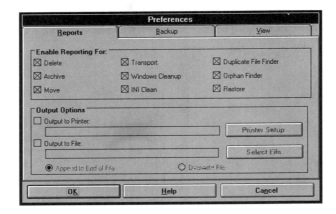

Reports Preferences

UnInstaller makes it easy for you to track the changes made during an uninstall session with its report-generation capability. UnInstaller provides reports for most actions and features. From the Reports options shown in Figure 14.2, you can specify which of the UnInstaller features, when used, will cause UnInstaller to generate reports. You can also specify whether to send the report to a file or to a printer. To set the Reports options, select the Reports tab.

Backup Preferences

To set the Backup options, select the Backup tab. From the Backup options shown in Figure 14.3, you can specify the UnInstaller features that will automatically create backups. When a backup is created, you can use the Restore feature to restore any changes made. The Security Delete feature allows you to specify whether the data in a deleted file is overwritten. Overwriting data in a deleted file prevents anyone from viewing the contents of the deleted file using special utilities.

View Preferences

To set the View options, select the View tab. From the View options shown in Figure 14.4, you can specify the way that UnInstaller interacts with the user (this means you). You can choose to hide or display the button bar (or toolbar), the status bar, and tips. You can also choose which operations you want to confirm. When confirmations are enabled, you will be prompted with a dialog box to confirm the action or operation.

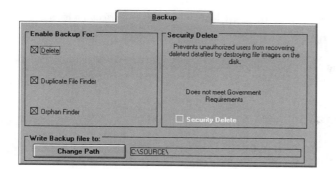

Fig. 14.3
The Backup file tab options.

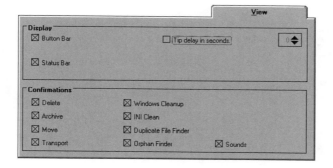

Fig. 14.4
The View options.

From Here...

Now that you are familiar with UnInstaller 3.0 and its features, you are ready to learn how to use UnInstaller.

■ Chapter 15, "Uninstalling Applications with UnInstaller 3.0," teaches you to how to use UnInstaller and its features to uninstall applications and clean up your system.

■ Chapter 16, "Using Archive Applications," teaches you how to compress and store applications you seldom use.

■ Chapter 17, "Using Transport Applications," discusses how you can move an application and all of its associated files and settings to another computer.

■ Chapter 18, "Using Move Applications," teaches you how to move an existing application to another directory or drive.

■ Chapter 19, "Using Windows Cleanup," covers the Windows Cleanup feature and how it enables you to quickly locate, view, and remove dozens of unnecessary files on your system.

- Chapter 20, "Using INIClean," teaches you how to locate, view, and edit any initialization files on your system.

- Chapter 21, "Using Duplicate File Finder," teaches you how to use the Duplicate File Finder to locate and remove duplicate files.

- Chapter 22, "Using Orphan Finder," explains the Orphan Finder feature and how you use it to locate orphan files.

- Chapter 23, "Using Disk Data," discusses the Disk Data feature and how you use it to view the contents of a drive or directory.

Chapter 15

Uninstalling Applications with UnInstaller 3.0

UnInstaller offers many features that you can use to uninstall applications and clean up your system. So far in this book you have learned to use the four-step uninstall process to remove applications with standard Windows components. In this chapter, you'll see how you can use UnInstaller 3.0 and its many features in the four-step uninstall process.

In this chapter, you learn to

- Use UnInstaller in the four-step uninstall process

- Use UnInstaller's Delete Applications feature to remove applications

- Use UnInstaller to clean up your system

Step 1: Preparing Your System

In Chapter 5, you learned that you need some preparation to have a success-ful uninstall session. This is true whether you are using the standard Win-dows components or UnInstaller. However, with UnInstaller you will find that the preparation phase is quicker and, in most cases, optional.

Getting System Information

When you are using UnInstaller, review the following before you start uninstalling applications and files:

- Initialization Files

- Fonts

- File Associations

Reviewing Your Initialization Files

The initialization files on your system contain a lot of useful, although hard to understand, information. Take a few minutes to review the sections in your WIN.INI and SYSTEM.INI files, then compare these sections with the sections described in Chapter 12, "Working with Initialization Files," which contains more information on sections in the .INI files. The more you know and understand about your Windows initialization files, the less likely you are to make mistakes when editing them.

UnInstaller automatically reviews your initialization files and determines the changes that need to be made. These changes are presented to you in the list of items that UnInstaller has marked for removal during the deletion process. Keep in mind that it is *your* decision whether items are deleted. The more you know, the better off you'll be.

Reviewing Your Fonts

Fonts can take up a lot of hard disk space and waste system resources. Using the Control Panel Fonts applet, review your list of installed fonts and determine which fonts you want to keep. As an alternative to the Fonts applet, you can use UnInstaller's Windows Cleanup feature to locate and review the fonts that are installed on your system. Make a note of any font that you want to delete.

Reviewing File Associations

Review the file associations defined in the WIN.INI file. You can do this easily with UnInstaller's Windows Cleanup feature. See Chapter 19, "Using Windows Cleanup," to view the file associations in the WIN.INI file. As you review the file associations, make sure that the associations are defined as you want them. UnInstaller uses the file associations to suggest the document files that should be deleted with an application.

For example, let's say you use the .DOC file extension for all of your Write documents instead of the default .WRI file extension. Let's also assume that you have Word for Windows installed. The file associations in your WIN.INI file, by default, indicate that the document files for Write have the .WRI extension and the document files for Word for Windows have the .DOC file extension. Therefore, if you delete Word for Windows, your Write documents will be marked for deletion. This happens because UnInstaller uses the file associations in the WIN.INI file to determine which document files to remove with an application. If you aren't careful to review the files marked for deletion, you can delete your Write documents by mistake. Similarly, if you delete Write, UnInstaller will not be able to locate your Write documents because you used a file extension that was not defined as a file association in the WIN.INI file. Reviewing your file associations helps you to prevent problems during the uninstall process.

Creating the BOOTLOG.TXT File

Even with UnInstaller, it is a good idea to create the BOOTLOG.TXT file. Review this step in Chapter 5, "Step 1: Preparing Your System."

Reviewing the Windows Files

Although UnInstaller will not list vital Windows files or Windows components when you uninstall applications, you need to be familiar with the basic structure of Windows, the Windows components, and various types of files that Windows uses. Review Chapter 5, "Step 1: Preparing Your System," for more information.

Moving and Organizing Your Files and Directories

Take a few minutes to review your directories and files. You can use UnInstaller's Disk Data feature to do this. Disk Data allows you to view the files and directories on any local drive. Disk Data provides information about each file, directory, and drive so you can easily determine the drives and directories that are taking up the most space on your hard drive(s).

Review the overall directory tree structure of your drives to determine whether you want to move applications and their files or directories. If you want to move an application, use UnInstaller's Move Applications feature to move an application, all of its files, and all of its settings to another drive or directory on your system.

See Chapter 18, "Using Move Applications," for information about the Move Applications feature. See Chapter 23, "Using Disk Data," for information about Disk Data.

Backing Up Your System

It is always a good idea to back up your system before an uninstall session. As a minimum, back up your initialization files. Optimally, you should back up your entire system.

Initialization Files

Before you use UnInstaller to uninstall an application, create a backup copy of your WIN.INI, SYSTEM.INI, AUTOEXEC.BAT, and CONFIG.SYS files. Copy these to a floppy and keep the floppy in a safe place. If you have problems after an uninstall session, use your backups to restore these files.

Application Directory

With UnInstaller, you really don't have to create a backup of your application directory. To be able to restore an application that you are uninstalling, make sure you have enabled backups for the Delete feature using the UnInstaller Preferences window.

WINDOWS Directory

If you don't have your original Windows installation disks, make a backup copy of your WINDOWS directory. If you have problems after an uninstall session, it may be necessary to use the backup to restore Windows to a working configuration.

Tip

The Delete Applications feature can automatically create a backup of all deleted files. To enable automatic backups for the Delete Applications feature, use the UnInstaller Preferences window. With automatic backups, you can restore your system if you accidentally delete a vital file.

Your Hard Drive

Backing up your hard drive regularly is a good idea. This not only allows you to restore your system if you make a mistake during an uninstall session, it also protects your data in case your hard drive crashes.

Step 2: Removing Application Files

In this step, you delete the application's files and program item or group. In Chapter 6, you used File Manager and Program Manager to complete this task. However, with UnInstaller you use the Delete Applications feature. The Delete Applications feature allows you to delete the application files, remove the program item or group, and remove all application settings and references from the Windows initialization files. In other words, UnInstaller's Delete Applications feature does everything necessary to completely remove all traces of an application.

To use UnInstaller's Delete Applications feature to remove an application, follow these steps:

1. Choose UnInstall, Delete Applications from the UnInstaller menu, or click the Delete Applications button from the UnInstaller toolbar. The Delete Applications window is displayed as shown in Figure 15.1.

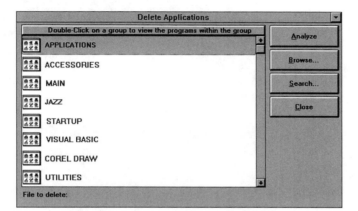

Fig. 15.1
The Delete Applications window.

2. On the left side of the Delete Applications window, you find a list of program groups. Locate the program group that contains the application to remove and double-click on the group icon. The applications in the group are listed.

3. Click the icon for the application that you want to delete.

> **Note**
>
> If you can't find the application that you are looking for by viewing the applications through the program groups, you can use the Browse and Search buttons to select an application to delete. The Browse button displays a standard file dialog box to help you locate the application file that you are looking for and is useful when searching for DOS and Windows applications not listed in your Windows shell.
>
> The Search button searches your hard drive for Windows applications that aren't listed in your Windows shell and presents you with a list of located applications. You can then select from the Windows applications that are found.
>
> The Search and Browse buttons are found in many of the UnInstaller features including Move Applications, Transport Applications, and Archive Applications.

4. Click the Analyze button. UnInstaller then performs its analysis of the application and determines the changes that need to be made to your system.

> **Note**
>
> The Analyze button does not cause the application to be deleted. You can still cancel the operation after clicking the Analyze button.

5. Once UnInstaller has analyzed the application, the Delete Applications window is updated to display four tabs that represent delete options as shown in Figure 15.2.

Fig. 15.2
The Delete
Applications
options.

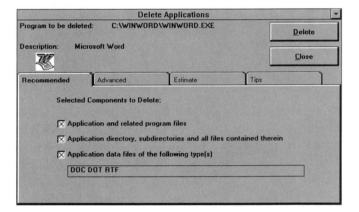

Tip
UnInstaller automatically checks the appropriate options in the Recommended tab. Although you can change these options, you should typically follow UnInstaller's suggestions for selecting application components to delete.

6. Click the Recommended tab. The Recommended tab options, as shown in Figure 15.2, allow you to specify which application components you want to delete. These options include:

- Application and related program files. This option must be clicked to delete the required files.

- Application directory, subdirectories, and all files contained therein. This option is good if you want to delete an entire application group. For example, many application packages that you buy are actually several applications. CorelDRAW! contains several applications including PHOTO-PAINT, CorelDRAW!, and CorelChart. If you want to delete all the applications in the application directory, click this button.

■ Application data files of the following type(s). This option is followed by one or more file extensions used by document files associated with the application. Click this option if you want to delete
any document files that UnInstaller finds.

7. Click the Advanced tab. The Advanced tab, as shown in Figure 15.3,
displays a detailed list of the files to be deleted. This tab also lists
entries in the system files (AUTOEXEC.BAT, CONFIG.SYS, WIN.INI,
SYSTEM.INI, etc.) that are to be removed when the application is
deleted.

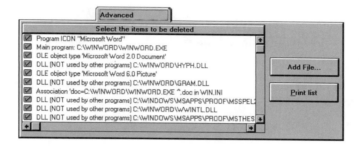

Fig. 15.3
The Advanced tab.

The items displayed in the Advanced tab are automatically marked by
UnInstaller using the following colors:

■ Green: These items are marked for deletion by UnInstaller.

■ Yellow: These items may be safely deleted, but be sure to review
them before they are deleted.

■ Red: These items are most likely used by other applications. If you
are uncertain if another application is using the item, don't allow
UnInstaller to delete it.

■ Blue: These items have been added by clicking the Add File button
in the Advanced tab.

■ Black: These items cannot be deleted because they are either in
use or on a read-only drive such as a CD-ROM.

8. Review the list of items displayed in the Advanced tab. You can change
the markings of an item by selecting it. Items that you want to delete
have a check mark in the items icon (refer to Fig. 15.3).

You can click the Add File button to add files to the list of items to be deleted. You can also use the Print List button to print the list of items to a file, printer, or both depending on the settings you have selected using the UnInstaller Preferences window.

9. Select the Estimate tab. The Estimate tab displays the amount of disk space that will be freed by deleting the application along with the number of files that will be deleted.

10. Select the Tips tab to get overview information about deleting applications.

11. Click the Delete button after setting all of your tab options. As UnInstaller prepares to delete application files and settings, you will be asked to confirm the delete operations (unless you have disabled Confirmations using UnInstaller Preferences).

UnInstaller provides you with the following buttons when asking you to confirm a delete operation:

- Yes: Deletes the specified file.

- Yes to All: Deletes all the files selected in the Advanced tab without individual confirmations.

- No: Does not delete the specified file.

- Cancel: Cancels the Delete Applications process.

- View: Allows you to view the contents of a file before deleting it.

Step 3: Editing Your Initialization Files

When you use UnInstaller's Delete Applications feature to uninstall an application, UnInstaller automatically makes the changes that need to be made to your SYSTEM.INI and WIN.INI files. In addition, it automatically locates and removes any private initialization files used by the application.

Although UnInstaller automatically handles the initialization files when uninstalling an application, you still need to review the SYSTEM.INI, WIN.INI, AUTOEXEC.BAT, and CONFIG.SYS files for any unnecessary information. Even though UnInstaller modifies these files, it does not remove information left from applications that you previously uninstalled manually or any other extraneous information.

Reviewing and Modifying SYSTEM.INI

Review the SYSTEM.INI file for extraneous information using UnInstaller's INIClean feature. INIClean allows you to view each of the entries and sections in the file and modify any entry.

Reviewing and Modifying WIN.INI

Review the WIN.INI file for unneeded sections and entries using UnInstaller's INIClean feature. INIClean allows you to view each of the entries and sections in the file and modify any entry.

Reviewing CONFIG.SYS

UnInstaller reviews the CONFIG.SYS file and makes changes, if necessary, during an uninstall session. However, review the CONFIG.SYS file to make sure that all appropriated changes were made. You can use Notepad or SysEdit to edit the CONFIG.SYS file.

Reviewing AUTOEXEC.BAT

Many applications make changes to the AUTOEXEC.BAT file. When an application is uninstalled, UnInstaller automatically removes changes to the AUTOEXEC.BAT file made by the application. However, use Notepad or SysEdit to review the AUTOEXEC.BAT file for extraneous information.

Step 4: Cleaning Up

Once you have deleted an application, you can use some of UnInstaller's other features to remove unwanted and unnecessary files from your hard drive.

Removing Unused, Unnecessary, and Outdated Files

UnInstaller provides the Windows Cleanup feature to remove several different types of unnecessary files from your hard drive. These file types are as follows:

Backup files	MS-DOS support programs
Clip art	Screensavers
Display drivers	Setup files
DOS support files	Sound files
Fonts	Standard mode files
Help files	Temp files
Lost cluster files	Text files
MIDI files	Wallpaper files
Miscellaneous files	Zip files
MS-DOS backup files	

For a description of each of these files, see Chapter 19, "Using Windows Cleanup."

When you start Windows Cleanup, it searches your hard drive(s) and locates all of the file types mentioned in this section. You have the option of viewing each file and archiving or deleting the files that you don't use. For example, you could delete the clip art files that you don't use and archive the ones that you do. Later, if you need to use an archived clip art file, you can use the Restore feature to restore the archived file so you can use it. Deleting or archiving these unnecessary files can save you a lot of hard disk space.

You can also use UnInstaller's Duplicate File Finder feature to locate and remove duplicate files from your system. See Chapter 21 for more information on using Duplicate File Finder.

Removing Unwanted Windows Components

Windows installs many utilities and accessories on your system. If you don't use one of the Windows utilities or accessories, you can delete it using UnInstaller's Delete Applications feature. You delete Windows utilities and accessories the same way that you delete any other application. Refer to "Step 2: Removing Application Files," in this chapter for more information about the Delete Applications feature.

Removing Temporary Files

After removing an application and cleaning your system, you need to exit Windows and return to the C:\ prompt so that you can delete any temporary files that Windows has left on your system. UnInstaller removes some of these files but does not remove any files that have the current date. It does this to avoid deleting any files that may be in use.

To delete the temporary files on your system, go to your WINDOWS and TEMP directories and delete the .TMP files that you find there. The TEMP directory is defined in your AUTOEXEC.BAT file by the SET TEMP command.

Caution

Do not delete temporary files when Windows is running because doing so will crash Windows. Be sure to exit Windows first.

Defragging Your Hard Drive

It is always a good idea to defragment your hard drive after uninstalling applications and removing files either manually or with UnInstaller 3.0. This will improve the performance of your system because DOS doesn't have to work as hard when reading files. Third-party applications, such as Norton Utilities and PC Tools, as well as the DOS DEFRAG utility, can be used to defragment your hard drive.

Now you're done. Reboot and test your system. If you have problems with Windows or Windows applications after uninstalling with UnInstaller, you should be able to restore the changes that you made. You can use the Restore feature to restore the changes, assuming that you enabled the appropriate Backups using UnInstaller Preferences.

From Here...

Now that you know how to perform an uninstall session with UnInstaller 3.0, you are ready to learn to use the other UnInstaller 3.0 features.

- Chapter 16, "Using Archive Applications," teaches you how to use UnInstaller's Archive Applications feature to compress and store applications you seldom use.

- Chapter 17, "Using Transport Applications," teaches you how to use UnInstaller's Transport Applications feature to move an entire application to another computer.

- Chapter 18, "Using Move Applications," teaches you how to use UnInstaller's Move feature to move an existing application to another directory or hard drive.

■ Chapter 19, "Using Windows Cleanup," teaches you how to use UnInstaller's Windows Cleanup feature to locate and remove dozens of unnecessary files on your system.

■ Chapter 20, "Using INIClean," teaches you how to use UnInstaller's INIClean feature to locate and edit initialization files on your system.

■ Chapter 21, "Using Duplicate File Finder," teaches you how to use UnInstaller's Duplicate File Finder feature to locate and delete duplicate files.

■ Chapter 22, "Using Orphan Finder," teaches you how to use UnInstaller's Orphan Finder feature to identify and remove orphaned files.

■ Chapter 23, "Using Disk Data," teaches you how to use UnInstaller's Disk Data feature to view the contents of a drive or directory.

Chapter 16

Using Archive Applications

UnInstaller provides the Archive Applications feature to archive an application and all of its files and settings.

In this chapter, you learn to

- Use the Archive Applications feature to archive applications
- Restore archived applications

Learning about Archive Applications

UnInstaller's Archive Applications feature allows you to archive applications that you seldom use. When UnInstaller archives an application, it locates all the files associated with the application, compresses the files, and stores the files in a single file called an archive file.

Archiving a file is very useful when you want to store an application and data that you may need to access later on. Let's say, for example, that you are changing over to a new spreadsheet program. Although the new spreadsheet program claims that it will import your old spreadsheets, you want to keep your old spreadsheet program on your system—just in case you have problems.

With UnInstaller's Archive Applications feature, you can keep your old spreadsheet program on your hard drive without taking up a lot of space, or you can store your application on floppies. By archiving your old spreadsheet program, the archived application will only take up a fraction of the space occupied by the original, unarchived application. If you ever need to use the old spreadsheet program, simply double-click the application's icon and UnInstaller will automatically extract and decompress your original spreadsheet application files.

Now let's look at how you can archive an application using the Archive Applications feature.

Archiving Applications

To use UnInstaller's Archive Applications feature for archiving an application, follow these simple steps:

1. Click the Archive Applications button from the UnInstaller toolbar or choose <u>U</u>nInstall, <u>A</u>rchive Applications from the UnInstaller menu.

2. The Archive Applications window is displayed as shown in Figure 16.1. It lists all available program groups on the left side of the window and provides four buttons—<u>A</u>nalyze, <u>B</u>rowse, <u>S</u>earch, and <u>C</u>lose.

Fig. 16.1
The Archive Applications window.

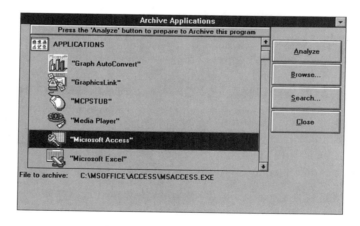

Tip
If you can't find the application that you are looking for through the program groups list box, you can use the <u>B</u>rowse and <u>S</u>earch buttons to select an application to archive.

3. Scroll through the program groups list box to locate the program group that contains the application you want to archive and double-click it. UnInstaller lists the applications contained in the program group.

4. Highlight the application you want to archive by clicking the application icon and then clicking the Analyze button. You are presented with four file tabs representing Archive options as shown in Figure 16.2.

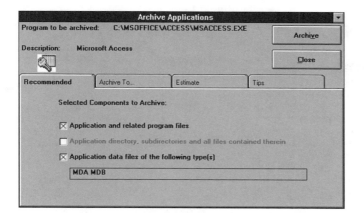

Fig. 16.2
The Archive
Applications
options.

5. Click the Recommended file tab. The Recommended tab options, as shown in Figure 16.2, allow you to specify which application components you want to archive. These options include:

- Application and related program files. This option must be checked to archive the required application files.

- Application directory, subdirectories, and all files contained therein. This option is good if you want to archive an entire application group. For example, many application packages like CorelDRAW! contain several applications such as CorelDRAW!, PHOTO-PAINT, and CorelChart. If you want to archive all the applications, click this button.

- Application data files of the following types. This option is followed by one or more file extensions used by document files associated with the application. Choose this option if you want to archive any document files that UnInstaller finds.

6. Click the Archive To file tab. The Archive To tab options, as shown in Figure 16.3, allow you to select the path for the archive, enter a name for the archive, and enter a description for the archive. UnInstaller provides default values for these options.

The Archive To file tab also provides the Add File button. The Add File button is great if you want to include any additional files in the archive. The file does not have to be associated with the application. The Set Path button allows you to define the path of the resulting archive file.

Tip
UnInstaller automatically checks the appropriate options in the Recommended tab. Although you can change these options, you should typically follow UnInstaller's suggestions for selecting application components to delete.

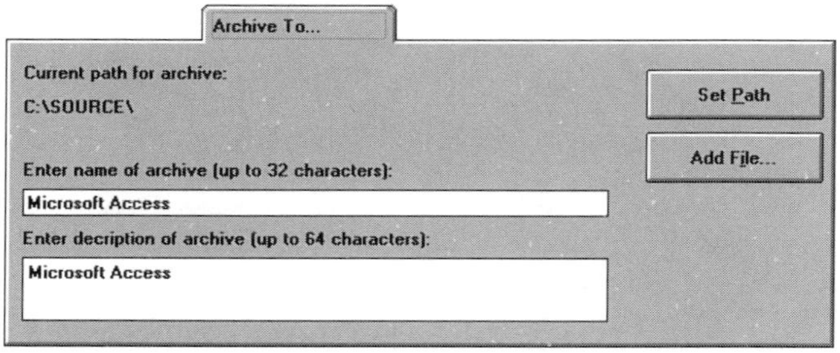

Fig. 16.3

The Archive To file tab options.

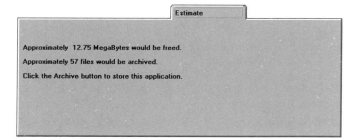

7. Click the Estimate file tab to get information about the archive operation before you proceed. The Estimate tab, as shown in Figure 16.4, shows the amount of disk space freed by the operation and the number of files that are to be archived.

Fig. 16.4

The Estimate file tab option.

Estimate

Approximately 12.75 MegaBytes would be freed.

Approximately 57 files would be archived.

Click the Archive button to store this application.

8. Click the Tips file tab if you would like helpful pointers, or tips, on archiving applications.

9. Once you have set all the desired options, click the Archive button to begin the archive operation. As a part of the archive operation, UnInstaller replaces the old program icon with a new icon. The new icon is a revised copy of the old icon. The new icon has a caution box placed around it and has the UnInstaller Archive label. This makes it easy to distinguish between normal application icons and archived application icons.

Once you have archived an application, you can restore it using UnInstaller's Restore feature.

Restoring Archived Applications

UnInstaller makes it easy to restore an archived application. Follow these steps to restore an application that you have archived using UnInstaller's Archive Applications feature:

1. Locate the icon for the archived application. It can be found in the original application's program group.

2. Double-click the icon for the archived application. UnInstaller is automatically launched and the Restore window, as shown in Figure 16.5, is opened and initialized with the appropriate information from the archived application.

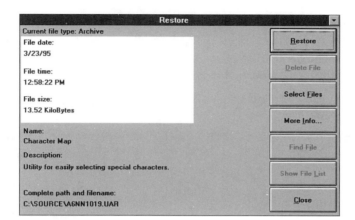

Fig. 16.5
The Restore window.

3. Click the Restore button.

4. UnInstaller asks you to confirm the Restore operation. Click Yes. UnInstaller then restores all the files in the archive and restores the original application icon.

5. UnInstaller then asks you whether you want to delete the archive icon created by the archive operation. If you choose yes, the archive icon and the archive file will be deleted. Otherwise, these will be left on your system.

From Here...

Now that you know how to archive applications using UnInstaller's Archive Applications and Restore features, you are ready to learn how to use the Transport Applications feature to move applications between computers.

■ Chapter 17, "Using Transport Applications," teaches you how to transport applications from one computer to another.

■ Chapter 18, "Using Move Applications," teaches you how to move applications to another drive or directory.

■ Chapter 19, "Using Windows Cleanup," teaches you how to remove unnecessary files from your system.

■ Chapter 20, "Using INIClean," teaches you how to review and edit initialization files.

■ Chapter 21, "Using Duplicate File Finder," teaches you how to locate and remove duplicate files on your system.

■ Chapter 22, "Using Orphan Finder," teaches you how to locate, remove, and reconnect orphaned files.

■ Chapter 23, "Using Disk Data," teaches you how to view your drives, directories, and files.

Chapter 17

Using Transport Applications

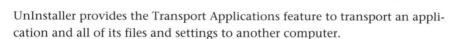

UnInstaller provides the Transport Applications feature to transport an application and all of its files and settings to another computer.

In this chapter, you learn to

- ■ Transport applications using the Transport Applications feature
- ■ Restore transported applications

Learning about the Transport Applications Feature

UnInstaller's Transport Applications feature is very useful for moving an application from one computer system to another. For example, if you want to transport an application that you have at work to your home computer, you can use the Transport Applications feature to take the application home with you. This feature is especially useful if you don't have the original installation disks.

The Transport Applications feature is very interesting because it moves all the files associated with an application. Using UnInstaller's capability to determine which files are associated with applications, the Transport Applications feature can effectively copy all related files including files not found in the application directory such as library files and group files. Transport Applications is also capable of capturing all the settings and user preferences for the application and transporting those settings to the destination computer. When you transport an application, however, the original application is not removed.

Using the Transport Applications feature involves two steps. The first step is to transport the application to a transport medium. The transport medium is the storage device that you use to store the information taken from the source system. The second step involves removing the information from the transport medium and placing it onto the destination system.

> **Caution**
>
> Although the Transport Applications feature makes transporting applications easy even without the original distribution disks, read the software licensing agreement provided with the application you are transporting for information regarding multiple copies of the same software. Some applications let you use the same application on two computers being used exclusively by the same person (for example, your office computer and laptop).

Now that you understand how and when to use Transport Applications, let's look more closely at the two procedures that you will need to follow to transport an application.

Transporting Applications

The first step in transporting applications between computers is to transport the application from the source computer system to some transport medium. The medium that you will most likely use is one or more floppy disks because these are used by almost all computer systems. However, if you are moving an application from one networked computer to another on the same network, you can use the network drive as your transport medium. Of course, you can also use any other device that is compatible with both systems (removable hard drives, optical drives, or whatever).

To transport an application from the source system to a transport medium, follow these steps:

1. Click the Transport Applications button from the UnInstaller toolbar or choose UnInstall, Transport Applications from the UnInstaller menu.

2. The Transport window is displayed as shown in Figure 17.1. The Transport window lists all available program groups on the left side of the window and provides four buttons—Analyze, Browse, Search, and Close.

3. Using the program groups listed on the left side of the Transport window, double-click the program group that contains the application you want to transport. UnInstaller lists the applications that are contained in the program group.

4. Highlight the application you want to transport by clicking the application icon. Click the Analyze button. You are presented with four file tabs representing Transport options as shown in Figure 17.2.

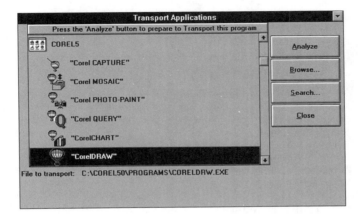

Fig. 17.1
The Transport window.

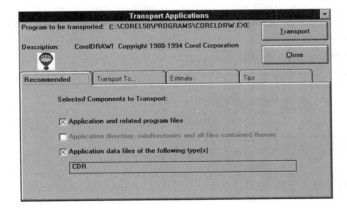

Fig. 17.2
The Transport options.

Tip
UnInstaller automatically checks the appropriate options in the Recommended tab. Although you can change these options, you should typically follow UnInstaller's suggestions for selecting application components to delete.

5. Click the Recommended file tab. The Recommended tab options, as shown in Figure 17.3, allow you to specify which application components you want to transport. These options include:

■ Application and related program files. This option must be checked to transport the required files.

■ Application directory, subdirectories, and all files contained therein. This option is good if you want to transport an entire application group. For example, many application packages that you buy are actually several applications. If you want to transport all the applications, select this button.

■ Application data files of the following type(s). This option is followed by one or more file extensions used by document files associated with the application. Choose this option if you want to transport any document files that UnInstaller finds.

Fig. 17.3
The Recommended file tab options.

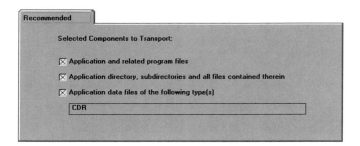

6. Click the Transport To file tab. The Transport To tab options, as shown in Figure 17.4, allow you to select the drive where the files will be copied for transport (i.e., the transport medium). If you are moving the files to another computer, you will probably use your floppy drive as the transport medium. UnInstaller will copy the files to the floppy disk and prompt you whenever you need to insert another disk.

Fig. 17.4
The Transport To file tab options.

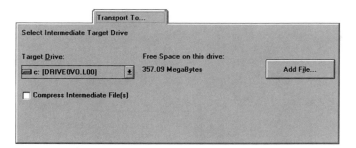

You can enable data compression by checking the Compress Intermediate File(s) check box. This allows you to get more files on each floppy (if you are using floppy disks for the transport) and reduce the overall size of the transport file.

The Transport To file tab also provides the Add File button. The Add File button is great if you want to include any additional files in the transport not found in the application directory. For example, this would come in handy if you want to move your favorite screensaver module while you're transporting your word processor.

7. Click the Estimate file tab to get information about the transport operation before you proceed. The Estimate tab, as shown in Figure 17.5, shows the amount of disk space required on the destination drive and the number of files that are to be transported.

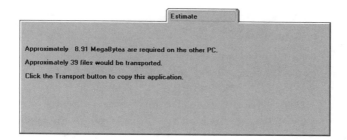

Fig. 17.5
The Estimate file tab.

8. Click the Tips file tab to get useful information on transporting applications.

9. Once you have set all the desired options, click the Transport button to begin the application transport.

Once you have transported an application to floppies (or some other transport medium), you are ready to restore the transported application onto the other computer system.

Restoring Transported Applications

The second step in transporting an application is to restore the transported files from the transport medium onto the destination system. The following steps can be used to restore a transported application onto the destination system:

1. Click the Restore button from the UnInstaller toolbar or choose UnInstall, Activate Transport. The Restore window appears as shown in Figure 17.6.

Fig. 17.6

The Restore window.

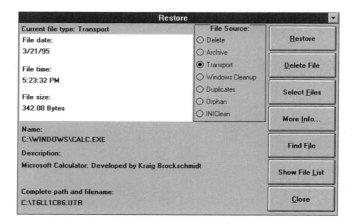

Tip

Uninstaller's Uninstall, Activate Transport and File, Restore menu items both activate the Restore feature. The only difference is in the way the Restore window is initialized. Depending on how the Restore window is invoked, you will be presented with different options and buttons.

2. In the File Source item, click Transport. A file dialog box appears. Select the drive and directory containing the transport file. Transport files have the .UTR file extension. Once you have selected the transport file, information about the transport file is displayed on the left side of the Restore window.

3. Click the Restore button. The Select Target Drive dialog box is displayed.

4. Select the target drive from the Select Target Drive dialog box and click OK.

5. UnInstaller asks you to confirm the Restore operation. Click Yes.

6. UnInstaller then copies all the files to the target drive. If the transported application has a program group and/or program item(s) associated with it, UnInstaller creates the program group and/or program item(s) during the Restore process.

From Here...

Now that you know how to transport applications between computers using UnInstaller's Transport Applications and Restore features, you are ready to learn how to use the Move feature to move applications to different drives or directories.

■ Chapter 18, "Using Move Applications," teaches you how to use UnInstaller's Move feature.

■ Chapter 19, "Using Windows Cleanup," teaches you how to use UnInstaller's Windows Cleanup feature.

■ Chapter 20, "Using INIClean," teaches you how to use UnInstaller's INIClean feature.

■ Chapter 21, "Using Duplicate File Finder," teaches you how to use UnInstaller's Duplicate File Finder feature.

■ Chapter 22, "Using Orphan Finder," teaches you how to use UnInstaller's Orphan Finder feature.

■ Chapter 23, "Using Disk Data," teaches you how to use UnInstaller's Disk Data feature.

Chapter 18

Using Move Applications

UnInstaller provides the Move Applications feature to move an application to another directory or drive.

In this chapter, you learn to

- Use the Move Applications feature
- Move applications

Learning about the Move Applications Feature

UnInstaller's Move Applications feature allows you to move applications around on your system. Have you ever needed to move an application to another drive on your system or network because you were running out of space on your main drive? Or maybe you wanted to move an application to another directory when you were organizing files. Whatever the case, the Move Applications feature moves an application and all the appropriate files while making all the modifications necessary to the system settings. The Move Applications feature is better than the standard copy utilities offered by DOS and File Manager because it moves the files and updates all the appropriate Windows and application settings to reflect the new location of the application.

Let's see how you can use UnInstaller to move an application.

Moving Applications

To move an application to another drive or directory, follow these simple steps:

1. Click the Move Applications button from the UnInstaller toolbar or choose Uninstall, Move Applications.

2. The Move window is displayed as shown in Figure 18.1. The Move window lists all available program groups on the left side of the window and provides four buttons—Analyze, Browse, Search, and Close.

Fig. 18.1
The Move window.

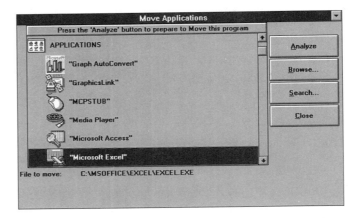

Tip
If you can't find the application that you are looking for by viewing the applications through the program groups, use the Browse and Search buttons to find the application you want to move.

3. Using the program groups listed on the left side of the Move window, double-click the program group that contains the application you want to move. UnInstaller lists the applications that are contained in the program group.

4. Highlight the application you want to move by clicking the application icon. Click the Analyze button. You will be presented with four file tabs representing Move options as shown in Figure 18.2.

5. Click the Recommended file tab. The Recommended tab options, as shown in Figure 18.2, allow you to specify which application components you want to move. These options include:

   ■ Application and related program files. This option must be checked to move the required files.

   ■ Application directory, subdirectories, and all files contained therein. This option is good if you want to move an entire application group. For example, many application packages that you buy are actually several applications. CorelDRAW! contains several applications including PHOTO-PAINT, CorelDRAW!, and CorelChart. If you want to move all the applications in the application directory, click this button.

■ Application data files of the following type(s). This option is followed by one or more file extensions used by document files associated with the application. Choose this option if you want to move any document files that UnInstaller finds.

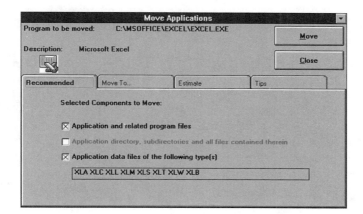

Fig. 18.2
Move options.

6. Click the Move To file tab. The Move To tab options, as shown in Figure 18.3, allow you to define the drive and path where the files will be moved.

   The Move To file tab also provides the Add File button. The Add File button is great if you want to move any additional files.

7. Click the Estimate file tab to get information about the move operation before you proceed. The Estimate tab, as shown in Figure 18.4, shows the overall size of the files being moved along with the number of files that are to be moved.

8. Click the Tips file tab to get useful information on moving applications.

9. Once you have set all the desired options, click the Move button to begin the move operation.

   UnInstaller moves the application to its new directory (creating directories if needed), makes changes to the appropriate Windows and application settings, verifies the moved files, and deletes the original files.

Tip
UnInstaller automatically checks the appropriate options in the Recommended tab. Although you can change these options, you should typically follow UnInstaller's suggestions for selecting application components to delete.

Fig. 18.3
The Move To file
tab options.

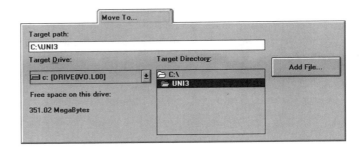

Fig. 18.4
The Estimate file
tab.

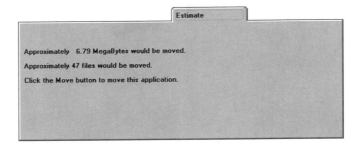

Caution

UnInstaller does not provide a way to recover a moved application. If you have problems with your application after moving it, move the application back to its original location. Moving the file back to its original location will fix any problem that you may have.

From Here...

Now that you know how to move applications using UnInstaller's Move Applications feature, you are ready to learn how to use the Windows Cleanup feature to remove unwanted files from your system.

- Chapter 19, "Using Windows Cleanup," teaches you how to locate, view, and remove unnecessary files.

- Chapter 20, "Using INIClean," teaches you how to locate, view, and edit initialization files using the INIClean feature.

- Chapter 21, "Using Duplicate File Finder," teaches you how to use the Duplicate File Finder feature to locate and remove duplicate files.

Chapter 19

Using Windows Cleanup

UnInstaller provides the Windows Cleanup feature to locate and remove unnecessary files from your system.

In this chapter, you learn to

- Use Windows Cleanup
- Locate and view extraneous files
- Delete unnecessary files

Learning about Windows Cleanup

UnInstaller's Windows Cleanup feature allows you to easily locate, view, and delete many types of files. Over time, files build up on your system. Many of these files are never used and can be removed from your system. Windows Cleanup knows the types of files that Windows uses and knows which types of files can be safely deleted.

When you run Windows Cleanup, it searches your system for several different types of files. The files listed in Table 19.1 are commonly copied to your system by various applications (and even by Windows) but are seldom used. You can safely delete these files without worrying about causing problems with Windows.

Table 19.1 Files for Windows Cleanup	
File Category	**Description**
Backup files	Backup files are created to preserve a file that is being changed. These files include files with the .BAK file extension, files that begin with WIN (with the exception of WIN.COM and WIN.INI), files that begin with SYSTEM (with the exception of SYSTEM.INI), files that begin with AUTOEXEC (with the exception of AUTOEXEC.BAT), and files that begin with CONFIG (with the exception of CONFIG.SYS).
Clip art	Clip art and graphics files are often installed with an application. If you don't use clip art, you can delete these files. Lists files with the .WMF, .PCX, .WPG, .CGM, .TIF, .GIF, .EPS, or .BMP file extensions. Files with the .BMP file extension found in the WINDOWS directory are not listed.
Display drivers	Display drivers are used by Windows to access your computer's display. When Windows is first installed, it automatically loads several generic display drivers. Display drivers listed in Windows Cleanup are not in use and can be safely deleted.
DOS support files	DOS support files allow Windows to run a DOS session while you are in Windows. If you do not run DOS applications from within Windows, you can safely delete these files.
Fonts	Windows Cleanup displays PostScript and TrueType fonts that are installed in Windows. If you don't use a font, you can delete its file.
Help files	Help files provide online help for an application. You can delete an application's help files if you don't use online help with the applications.
Lost cluster files	Lost cluster files are created by the CHKDSK and SCANDISK DOS programs when correcting lost clusters on your hard drive.
MIDI files	MIDI files are music files that can be played on most sound cards. If you don't play MIDI music on your system, you can delete these files. These files have the .MID file extension.
Miscellaneous files	Windows Cleanup locates several miscellaneous files installed with Windows including extra icon files and miscellaneous support files.
MS-DOS backup files	When you upgrade DOS, backup files are created. If the upgrade is operating properly, you can delete these backups.
MS-DOS support programs	MS-DOS support programs are installed by MS-DOS and seldom used. Windows Cleanup lists files that are not being used in your AUTOEXEC.BAT or CONFIG.SYS files. You can delete these files.

File Category	Description
Screensavers	Windows has a screensaver program built into it that supports special modules with the .SCR extension. If you don't use the Windows screensaver, you can delete these files.
Setup files	Applications typically store their files in a compressed format on the installation diskettes. During installation, most install programs copy these compressed files to your hard drive, decompress them, and delete the compressed copies. Windows Cleanup locates compressed files left on your system. You can safely delete these files. These files have an underscore character (_) at the end of the file extension. The underscore character indicates a compressed file used in setup routines.
Sound files	Wave (.WAV) files can be played with your sound card. However, these files take up a lot of space. Delete any of these files that you don't need.
Standard mode files	Windows operates in either of two modes: standard or 386 enhanced mode. You can delete these files if you run Windows only in 386 enhanced mode.
Temp files	Windows and Windows applications use temporary files to store information while the application is running. Windows Cleanup lists temporary files with the .TMP file extension that are at least one day old.
Text files	Text files can be found in almost every application directory. Windows Cleanup locates these text files with the .DIZ, .TXT, .WRI, or .SDI file extensions and allows you to delete them.
Wallpaper files	Wallpaper files are .BMP files that can be used to display an image on the Windows Desktop. Windows Cleanup locates these files and allows you to delete those that you don't use.
Zip files	.ZIP files are compressed files using the ZIP format developed by PKWare. Windows Cleanup locates these files and allows you to delete them.

With Windows Cleanup, you can view the files in each of the file categories and determine which files you want to delete. If you don't want to delete them because you think you might need them in the future, you can archive them to save space on your hard drive.

Windows Cleanup is easy to use and allows you to quickly delete and/or archive unnecessary files. Let's see how you can use Windows Cleanup to clean up your files.

Removing Unnecessary Files

Everybody's system has files on it that aren't needed. Windows Cleanup provides an easy way for you to locate and remove excess files. To use Windows Cleanup, follow these simple steps:

1. Click the Windows Cleanup button from the UnInstaller toolbar or choose Cleanup, Windows Cleanup from the UnInstaller menu. The Windows Cleanup window is displayed as shown in Figure 19.1.

2. Click the Cleanup file tab. This section displays several categories of files that have been located on your hard drive along with the total size of the files that were found in each file category.

Fig. 19.1
The Windows Cleanup window.

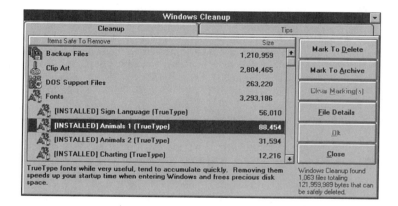

3. To view the files in each category, double-click the appropriate file category. The files are listed beneath the file category name. Once the files have been listed you can view the file, mark it for deletion, or mark it for archiving.

4. To view the contents of a file, double-click the appropriate filename. UnInstaller opens a window that either displays the contents of the file or provides file information. The type of window that is displayed depends on the type of file you select. Close the window when you have finished viewing the file.

5. To mark a file for deletion, select the file by clicking the filename. Click the Mark To Delete button. This button adds the file to the list of files that will be deleted. If you think that you may need the file later, you may consider archiving the file instead of deleting it. When a file is marked for deletion, the icon for the file is replaced with a trash can icon.

6. To mark a file for archiving, select the file by clicking the filename. Click the Mark To _A_rchive button. This button adds the file to the list of files that will be archived. When a file is marked for archiving, the icon for the file is replaced with an archive icon.

7. Once you have marked all the files that you want to delete and archive, click the _F_ile Details button. This option allows you to view all the files that you have currently selected.

> **Note**
>
> If you happen to select a file for deletion or archiving by mistake, you can deselect it by highlighting the file and clicking the Clear _M_arking(s) button.

8. After you have finalized your list of files to delete and/or archive, click OK.

9. Windows Cleanup asks you to confirm the actual deletion and archiving operations. Choose Yes to delete and/or archive the files.

> **Note**
>
> If you have archived files using Windows Cleanup, you can restore the archived files using UnInstaller's Restore feature.

Tip
You can restore deleted files if you have the _B_ackup option for the specified operation enabled in the Preferences window.

From Here...

Now that you know how to remove unwanted files from your computer using UnInstaller's Windows Cleanup feature, you are ready to learn how to use the INIClean feature to review and edit your initialization files.

- Chapter 20, "Using INIClean," teaches you how to use UnInstaller's INIClean feature.

- Chapter 21, "Using Duplicate File Finder," teaches you how to use UnInstaller's Duplicate File Finder feature.

- Chapter 22, "Using Orphan Finder," teaches you how to locate, remove, and reconnect orphaned files.

- Chapter 23, "Using Disk Data," teaches you how to view your drives, directories, and files.

Using INIClean

UnInstaller provides the INIClean feature to view and edit initialization files.

In this chapter, you learn to

- Use the INIClean feature
- Locate and view initialization files
- Edit entries in an initialization file

Learning about INIClean

UnInstaller's INIClean feature allows you to view and edit any initialization file on your system. As you recall from Chapter 12, "Working with Initialization Files," an initialization file is a special type of file used by Windows and Windows applications to store various types of information, including configurations, settings, passwords, user preferences, and so forth. When Windows is installed, several initialization files are copied to your system. These files are considered standard initialization files and are used by Windows and the standard Windows components.

Another type of initialization file that you'll find on your system is the private initialization file. Private initialization files are created and used exclusively by one application. You will likely find dozens of private initialization files on your system. An application uses a private initialization file to store information that it needs to operate.

With INIClean, you can view and edit the standard Windows initialization files as well as private initialization files. To use INIClean, you need to understand how initialization files are formatted. In Chapter 12, you learned that all Windows initialization files are formatted in the same way. Each initialization file is made up of sections and entries. Each section in an initialization file is formatted as follows:

[section]

entry=value

where

[section] is the name of the section. The section name is always enclosed in brackets.

entry is the name of a line in the section

value is any value assigned to the entry

Sections may contain one or more entries. The various sections of an initialization file can appear in any order.

INIClean provides several options that help you locate the initialization (.INI) file you want to edit. Once you have located the appropriate .INI file, you have the option to view any section and entry in the file. INIClean also provides an editing feature that allows you to edit entries in the .INI file. Let's see how you can use INIClean to locate, view, and edit .INI files.

Caution

Before editing any files with INIClean, be sure to make backups of those files.

Editing .INI Files

UnInstaller's INIClean feature allows you to quickly locate, view, and edit any initialization file. Follow these simple steps to use INIClean.

1. Click the INIClean button from the UnInstaller toolbar or choose Cleanup, INIClean from the UnInstaller menu.

2. The INIClean window, as shown in Figure 20.1, is displayed. The window contains four file tabs that represent INIClean options.

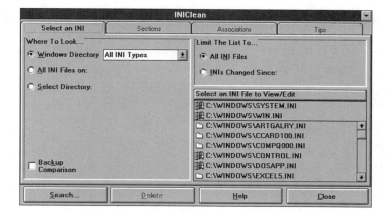

Fig. 20.1
The INIClean
window.

3. Click the Select an INI file tab. The Select an INI tab options, as shown in Figure 20.1, allow you to select a .INI file to view and edit. Several options are provided that control the .INI files that are listed for you to view. These options include the Where To Look and Limit The List To.

4. The Where To Look option allows you to specify where INIClean searches for .INI files. These options include Windows Directory, All INI Files on, and Select Directory.

   ■ Windows Directory. This option limits the search for .INI files to the WINDOWS directory. When this option is selected, a list box is displayed to the right of the option to allow you to select any of the following options:

     • All INI Types: All files with the .INI file extension found in the WINDOWS directory are listed.

     • Standard INIs: Only the standard Windows .INI files found in the WINDOWS directory are listed.

     • Non-Standard INIs: Only non-standard .INI files found in the WINDOWS directory are listed.

   ■ All INI Files on: This option opens the search for .INI files to an entire drive. When this option is selected, a drive list box is displayed to the right of the option to allow you to select the drive for the .INI file search.

■ Select Directory. This option limits the search for .INI files to a particular directory. When this option is selected, a drive list box and directory tree are displayed to the right of the Where To Look options. You can use the drive icon to specify the drive for the search and the directory tree to specify the directory for the search.

Select the appropriate option.

5. The Limit The List To options allow you to set search restrictions beyond those specified in Where To Look. These options include the following:

■ All INI Files. This option allows you to include all .INI files found.

■ INIs Changed Since. This options allows you to specify a date. When this option is selected, a date edit field is displayed that allows you to enter a date. Any .INI file that is older than the specified date will not be included in the .INI file search.

Select the appropriate option.

6. Once you have set the Where To Look and Limit the List To options, your list of .INI files is displayed in the lower right section of the Select an INI folder. Select the .INI file you want to review and/or edit by clicking once on the appropriate filename.

7. Click the Sections file tab. The Sections options, as shown in Figure 20.2, allow you to view and edit entries in the various sections of your .INI file.

Fig. 20.2
The Sections file tab options.

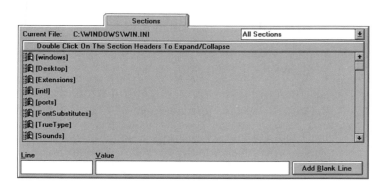

8. To view the entries in a section, double-click the section name. The entries in the section are listed beneath the section name.

9. To edit an entry in a section, highlight the entry that you want to edit by clicking once on the entry. The Line and Value edit fields at the bottom of the Sections folder display the information for the entry you selected. The Line edit field contains the key name for the entry. The Value edit field contains the value assigned to the key name. You can use these edit fields to modify an entry.

10. While you are in the Sections folder, you can use the following three INIClean buttons: Add Blank Line, Search, and Delete. The Search and Delete buttons are located at the bottom of the INIClean window.

- Add Blank Line. Clicking the Add Blank Line button inserts a blank line into the file. The blank line is inserted at the bottom of the current section. Blank lines are ignored by Windows but are useful to visually separate sections.

- Search: Clicking the Search button displays a search dialog box. You can enter text into the dialog box and INIClean attempts to locate that text in the .INI file.

- Delete: Clicking the Delete button deletes the highlighted line or section in the .INI file.

11. Click the Associations file tab. The Associations options, as shown in Figure 20.3, allow you view the file associations defined in your WIN.INI file.

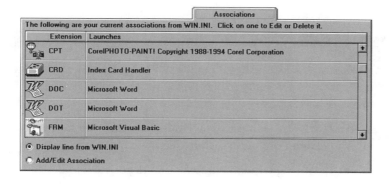

Fig. 20.3
The Associations file tab options.

12. The current associations in your WIN.INI file are displayed in alphabetical order. The file extension and application icon are displayed on the left. The Application name is displayed on the right. To select an association, simply click the appropriate line. When the Display line from WIN.INI option is selected, the actual line from the WIN.INI file is displayed to the right of the option.

13. To delete an association that exists in your WIN.INI file, simply select the association and click the <u>D</u>elete button (refer to Fig. 20.1). UnInstaller asks you to confirm the deletion. Choose Yes.

14. To add or edit an association to your WIN.INI file, select the Add/Edit Association option. When this option is selected, a file extension edit field, a Browse Files button, and a Browse Groups button are displayed.

- The file extension edit field enables you to enter the file extension for a new association or edit the extension for an existing association.

- The Browse Files button displays a file dialog box that allows you to search through your drives and directories for an application file to associate with the file extension in the file extension edit field.

- The Browse Groups button displays a window that lists the program groups on your system. You can search through your program groups to find the application that you want to associate with the file extension.

Caution
UnInstaller does not provide a way to undo changes made with INIClean. Use caution when making changes to any initialization file.

From Here...

Now that you know how to edit and modify initialization files using the INIClean feature, you are ready to learn how to use the Duplicate File Finder feature to locate and remove duplicate files on your system.

- Chapter 21, "Using Duplicate File Finder," teaches you how to locate and remove duplicate files on your system.

- Chapter 22, "Using Orphan Finder," teaches you how to use UnInstaller's Orphan Finder feature to locate and delete orphaned files.

- Chapter 23, "Using Disk Data," teaches you how to use UnInstaller's Disk Data feature to view files and directories on your system.

Using Duplicate File Finder

UnInstaller provides the Duplicate File Finder feature to locate and remove duplicate files on your system.

In this chapter, you learn to

- Define settings used to conduct duplicate file searches
- Use Duplicate File Finder to remove unwanted duplicate files

Learning about Duplicate File Finder

UnInstaller's Duplicate File Finder feature helps you locate and remove duplicate files. Many applications use common files, such as .DLLs and runtime modules, and each of these applications copies these common files to your system. Unless these applications are copying the files to the same directory, you are going to have duplicate files on your system.

As an example, Windows and DOS load many of the same files onto your system. DOS copies its files to the DOS directory while Windows copies its files to the WINDOWS directory. The result is wasted space on your hard drive.

The Duplicate File Finder feature is a helpful tool that searches your hard drive for duplicate files. It then provides you with a complete list of duplicate files. You have the option to view the files and delete any file you want. Let's take a look at how you can use Duplicate File Finder to locate (and even remove) duplicate files.

> **Caution**
>
> Be careful when removing duplicate files. Applications typically expect to find files in a particular location. If you are planning to remove a duplicate file, make sure the remaining file is in a directory defined in the DOS PATH statement, in the WINDOWS directory, or in the WINDOWS\SYSTEM directory.

Searching for Duplicate Files

The following steps can be used to locate, view, and optionally remove, duplicate files:

1. Click the Duplicate File Finder button from the UnInstaller toolbar or choose Cleanup, Duplicate File Finder from the UnInstaller menu. If this is the first time that you have used Duplicate File Finder, the Duplicate File Finder Settings window is displayed as shown in Figure 21.1. The window contains six file tabs that represent the options Duplicate File Finder uses to perform the duplicate file search.

> **Note**
>
> If this is not the first time you have used Duplicate File Finder, you will be taken to the File Listing window as shown in Figure 21.6. When the File Listing window is displayed, you can get to the Settings window by clicking the Settings button at the bottom of the window.

Fig. 21.1
The Settings window.

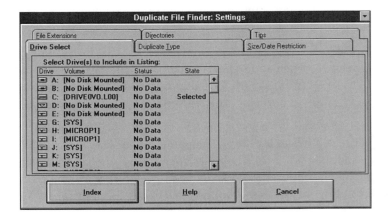

2. Choose the <u>D</u>rive Select file tab. The <u>D</u>rive Select file tab options, as shown in Figure 21.1, list the drives available on your system. You can select one or more drives to use by clicking the appropriate drive icon(s).

3. Choose the Duplicate <u>T</u>ype tab. The Duplicate <u>T</u>ype options, as shown in Figure 21.2, allow you to specify the type of Duplicate File Search that UnInstaller performs. These options follow:

■ Duplicate Filenames: When this option is selected, UnInstaller searches for files with duplicate filenames.

■ True Duplicates: When this option is selected, UnInstaller searches for files with the same filename, size, date, and time.

■ All files: When this option is selected, UnInstaller lists all files on the selected drive, sorted by filename.

Choose the option you desire.

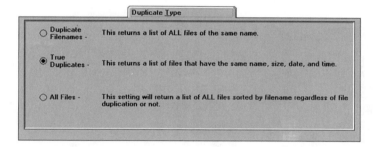

Fig. 21.2
Duplicate <u>T</u>ype options.

4. Choose the <u>S</u>ize/Date Restriction tab. The <u>S</u>ize/Date Restriction options, as shown in Figure 21.3, allow you to restrict the search for duplicate files by file size and/or file date.

■ The File Size Restriction option allows you to specify a file size to control the search for duplicate files. When this option is selected, UnInstaller only searches for files that are smaller, equal to, or larger than the specified size.

■ The File Date Restriction option allows you to specify the file date to control the search for duplicate files. When this option is selected, UnInstaller only searches for files that are dated before, on, or after the specified date.

Fig. 21.3
Size/Date Restric-
tion options.

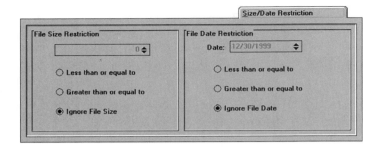

5. Choose the File Extensions tab. The File Extensions options, as shown in Figure 21.4, allow you to define a list of file extensions that you can include or exclude in UnInstaller's search for duplicate files.

To create a list of file extensions, simply choose either the Exclude List or Include List option, type the file extension, and click the Add button. You can add as many extensions to the extensions list as you want. Click the Remove button to remove an extension from the list.

Fig. 21.4
File Extensions
options.

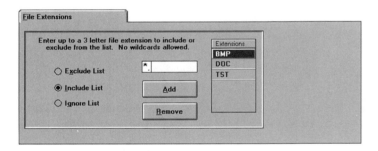

6. Choose the Directories tab. The Directories options, as shown in Figure 21.5, allow you to exclude certain directories and subdirectories from the search of duplicate files. If you want to use the directory exclusion feature, deselect the Don't Use Exclusion check box.

To build a list of excluded directories and subdirectories, locate the drive and directory using the directory tree on the left side of the window. Click the Add button to add a directory. Click the Add Subs button to add the directory and all of its subdirectories to the exclusion list.

If you need to remove items from the exclusion list, select the appropriate directory and click the Remove button. Click the Rmv All button to clear the list of excluded directories.

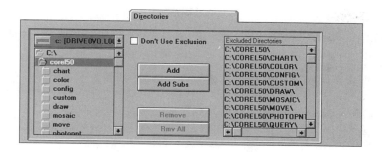

Fig. 21.5
The Directories
options.

7. Click the Tips file tab to get useful, overview information on Duplicate File Finder settings.

8. Once you have set all the duplicate file search options, click the Index button from the bottom of the Duplicate File Finder: Settings window. The Duplicate File Finder: File Listing window is displayed as shown in Figure 21.6. This window displays a listing of all your duplicate files using the search options you specified.

Fig. 21.6
The File Listing
window.

9. From the File Listing window, you have the four options as follows: Delete, Move, Rename, and View.

   ■ Delete: The Delete button deletes the selected file.

   ■ Move: The Move button moves the selected file to a new drive or directory.

   ■ Rename: The Rename button renames the selected file.

   ■ View: The View button opens the file for viewing.

You can also get file information and print the duplicate file listing.

If you want to change your search options, click the Settings button and you will be returned to the Settings window.

> **Note**
>
> If you have selected the Duplicate File Finder backup option from UnInstaller Preferences, you can restore any changes made with Duplicate File Finder. Open UnInstaller Preferences by clicking the Preferences button or choosing File, Preferences.

From Here...

Now that you have learned how to search for and locate duplicate files, you are ready to learn how to use Orphan Finder.

- Chapter 22, "Using Orphan Finder," teaches you how to locate, remove, and reconnect orphaned files.

- Chapter 23, "Using Disk Data," teaches you how to view your drives, directories, and files.

Chapter 22

Using Orphan Finder

UnInstaller's Orphan Finder allows you to easily find executable (.EXE) files that aren't referenced by Windows Program Manager and dynamic link library (.DLL) files that aren't used by any application programs.

In this chapter, you learn to

- Use Orphan Finder to locate orphaned files

- Delete orphaned files

- Reconnect orphaned files

Learning about Orphan Finder

Orphan finder helps you locate and remove orphaned files. An orphaned file is defined as

- An executable file (.EXE) that is not represented by an icon in Program Manager

- A dynamic link library (.DLL) file that UnInstaller is unable to associate with any executable file

Orphan Finder searches all the files on your hard drive and uses complex algorithms to determine whether a file is orphaned. Because orphaned files are useless and take up space on your hard drive, make every effort to delete all the orphaned files you can.

> **Caution**
>
> Even though Orphan Finder uses SmartLinks and other techniques to determine which files are truly orphaned files, Orphan Finder can, and does, make mistakes. Use extreme caution before deleting or reconnecting orphaned files. Remember, the final decision to delete a file is up to you.

There are three basic procedures that you need to be familiar with to use Orphan Finder. First, you need to be able to locate orphaned files. Once you have located the orphaned files, you'll need to delete or reconnect the orphaned files. You'll want to delete files that you don't want or need on your system. You'll want to reconnect orphaned .EXE files you want to keep. In the process of using Orphan Finder, you may find applications that you thought were long lost on your system. Reconnect these files so you can use them again. These three basic procedures are presented in the remainder of this chapter.

Locating Orphan Files

Before you can delete or reconnect orphaned files, you need to locate and view these files. The following steps create a list of orphaned files:

1. Click the Orphan Finder button from the UnInstaller toolbar, or choose Cleanup, Orphan Finder from the UnInstaller menu to start the Orphan Finder.

2. The Orphans Database dialog box may be displayed at this time. This dialog box is sometimes displayed when you try to perform an operation that uses the Orphans database and the database has not been updated.

   Allow UnInstaller to update the database at this time if this dialog box is displayed. UnInstaller uses the information in this database to make intelligent choices when finding orphaned files.

3. The Find Orphaned Files window is now displayed as shown in Figure 22.1.

4. The left side of the Find Orphaned Files window displays executable (.EXE) files that aren't connected to Program Manager. You can click any file in the list to select it. Once you have selected the executable file, you can delete or reconnect it.

5. The right side of the Find Orphaned Files window displays dynamic link library files (.DLLs) that are not associated with any executable files. You can click any of the files in the list to select it. Once you have selected a .DLL file, you can delete it.

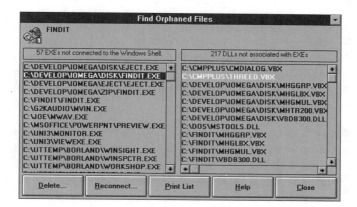

Fig. 22.1
The Find Orphaned Files window.

From the Find Orphaned Files window, you have the option to delete executable or .DLL files, reconnect executable files, or print a list of orphaned files.

Deleting Orphaned Files

Once you have obtained a list of orphaned files, you can delete any orphaned executable (.EXE) or dynamic link library (.DLL) file. Depending on what UnInstaller was able to determine about the orphaned file (associated files, purpose, file type, and so on), you may also be able to delete any files that are associated with the orphaned files. The following steps can be used with UnInstaller to delete orphaned files.

> **Note**
>
> If you have selected the Orphan Finder backup option from UnInstaller Preferences, you can restore any files deleted with Orphan Finder.

1. From the Find Orphaned Files window, select the .EXE or .DLL file(s) you want to delete.

2. Click the Delete button. The Delete Applications window is displayed as shown in Figure 22.2. You are presented with four file tabs representing Delete options.

Tip
UnInstaller auto-
matically checks
the appropriate
options in the
Recommended tab.
Although you can
change these op-
tions, you should
typically follow
UnInstaller's
suggestions for
selecting applica-
tion components
to delete.

3. Click the Recommended file tab. The Recommended tab options allow you to specify which application components you want to delete. These options include:

   ■ Application and related program files. This option must be checked to delete the identified files.

   ■ Application directory, subdirectories, and all files contained therein. This option is good if you want to delete an entire appli-cation group. For example, many application packages that you buy are actually several applications. If you want to delete all the applications, choose this option.

   ■ Application data files of the following type(s). This option is fol-lowed by one or more file extensions used by document files asso-ciated with the application. Choose this option if you want to delete any document files that UnInstaller finds.

Fig. 22.2
The Delete
Applications
window.

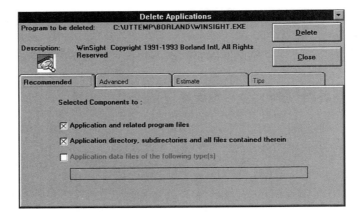

4. Click the Advanced tab as shown in Figure 22.3. The files marked for deletion are listed on the left side of the tab folder. From this file list, you can choose the files that you want to delete. If you do not want to delete a file, remove the check mark located beside the file by clicking the filename. You can also add files to the list of files marked for dele-tion by clicking the Add File button.

5. Click the Estimate file tab to get information about the delete operation before you proceed. The Estimate tab, as shown in Figure 22.4, shows the amount of disk space to be freed by the operation and the number of files that are to be deleted.

6. Click the Tips file tab to get useful information on deleting applications.

7. Click the Delete button. UnInstaller asks you to confirm the deletion of the files. Once you provide confirmation, the files are deleted.

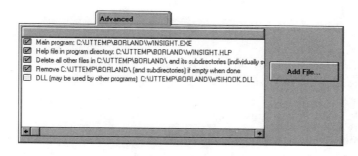

Fig. 22.3
The Advanced tab options.

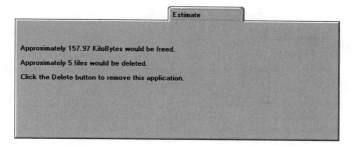

Fig. 22.4
The Estimate tab options.

8. Once the files have been deleted, UnInstaller updates the Orphans database and returns you to the Find Orphaned Files window.

Reconnecting Orphaned Files

Once you have obtained a list of orphaned files, you can reconnect any orphaned executable (.EXE) files to Program Manager. Orphan Finder creates a program item and places it in the program group of your choice. The following steps can be used with UnInstaller to reconnect orphaned files to the Windows shell (usually Program Manager):

1. From the Find Orphaned Files window, select the .EXE file that you want to reconnect to Program Manager.

2. Click the Reconnect button. The Add Item to Shell dialog box is displayed as shown in Figure 22.5.

Fig. 22.5
The Add Item to
Shell dialog box.

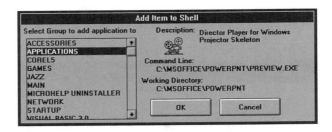

3. From the list of program groups provided, select a program group for the reconnected item. You can do this by clicking once on the appropriate group icon and then clicking OK. A program icon is created for the file in the appropriate program group.

4. Once the file has been reconnected to Program Manager, you are returned to the Find Orphaned Files window.

From Here...

Now that you know how to locate, delete, and reconnect orphaned files using UnInstaller's Orphan Finder feature, you are ready to learn how to use Disk Data to analyze your hard drive.

■ Chapter 23, "Using Disk Data," teaches you how to use the Disk Data window to view directories and files on your hard drive.

Chapter 23

Using Disk Data

UnInstaller provides the Disk Data feature to view the directories and files on your system's hard drive(s).

In this chapter, you learn to

- Use the Disk Data feature
- View the directories on a hard drive
- View the files in a directory

Learning about Disk Data

UnInstaller's Disk Data feature allows you to view the drives, directories, and files on your system or network. You can use Disk Data to determine the amount of space occupied on your hard drive(s), the cumulative size of a directory and all of its contents, and the size of a file. Disk Data uses graphical information bars to help you identify potential trouble spots on your hard drive.

UnInstaller's Disk Data feature uses three colors in its information bars to indicate the relative amount of space being used on a drive, in a directory, or by a file. The colors for the bars are red, yellow, and green. Red indicates large files and directories, yellow indicates medium-sized files and directories, and green indicates small files and directories.

Viewing Drive and Directory Information

UnInstaller's Disk Data feature allows you to view drive, directory, and file information. Follow these steps to use Disk Data:

1. Click the Disk Data button from the UnInstaller toolbar, or choose Cleanup, Disk Data from the UnInstaller menu. The Disk Data window is displayed as shown in Figure 23.1.

Fig. 23.1
The Disk Data window.

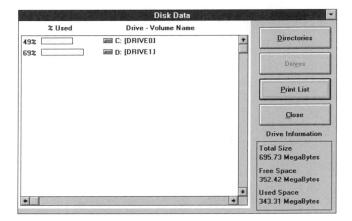

2. When the Disk Data window is first displayed, you will be presented with a list of drives that are available to your system. For each drive, a drive icon, volume name, and percentage value are listed. The percentage value indicates the amount of disk space that is currently occupied on the drive.

3. To view the contents of a drive, click the appropriate drive icon to select it, then click the Directories button.

Disk Data starts gathering information about the directories and files on your hard drive. This may take a few seconds or a few minutes depending on the size of the hard drive and the number of files on the drive.

4. The Disk Data window is updated, as shown in Figure 23.2, to display the directory structure of the selected hard drive. To the left of each directory icon is a value indicating the amount of space occupied by the directory, its subdirectories, and the files in the directory and subdirectories.

You can expand any directory to view its subdirectory by double-clicking the directory icon. Double-click an expanded directory to hide the subdirectory icons.

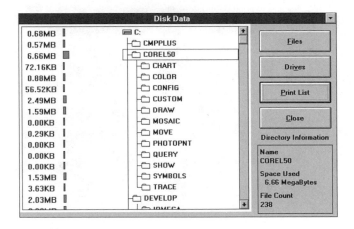

Fig. 23.2
The Disk Data
directories listing.

5. To view the files in a directory, select the directory and click the Files button. The Disk Data window is updated, as shown in Figure 23.3, to display the files of the selected directory. The files are listed in alphabetical order.

Each file is represented by a file icon, the filename, and file size. Disk Data also provides a colored bar that indicates the relative size of the file.

Note

When files are being displayed in the Disk Data window, the top button in the window is the Directories button. When directories are being displayed, however, the top button becomes the Files button.

6. To view the contents of a file or information about a file, simply double-click the file icon or filename. Disk Data opens the Viewer window, as shown in Figure 23.4, to display either the contents of the file, or detailed technical information about the file. The contents of the file are displayed for printable files while technical information about the file is displayed for non-printable files.

7. From the Disk Data window, you can click the Print List button to print the drive, directory, or file list currently being displayed.

Tip
If you want to make a quick determination about which drives, directories, and files are taking up the most space on your hard drive, look for the red information bars.

If you are viewing a directory or file listing, click the Dri_v_es button to return to the drives listing.

Fig. 23.3

The Disk Data files listing.

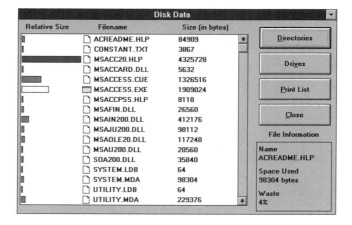

Fig. 23.4

The Viewer window.

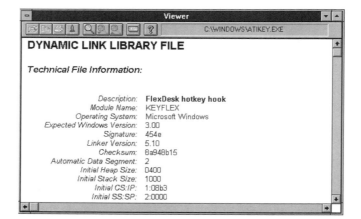

From Here...

Now that you know how to use Disk Data and all of the other UnInstaller features, you are ready to use UnInstaller to uninstall applications and to clean up your system.

■ Chapter 4, "Learning the Uninstall Process," explains the basic procedures for removing applications and application files from your system.

■ Chapter 14, "Learning about UnInstaller 3.0," introduces you to UnInstaller and its many features.

Crash Recovery Procedures

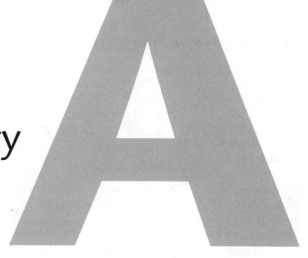

Whenever you uninstall applications or make changes to the Windows con-figuration files, there is a chance that you will cause some problems on your system. These problems can generally be fixed using simple techniques. In this appendix, we'll look at three levels of problems that you may encounter after uninstalling an application and/or cleaning up your system. These three levels, in order from most severe to least severe, are as follows:

- Your system won't boot

- Windows won't start

- One or more of your applications won't work

Let's look at some potential solutions to these problems.

Your System Won't Boot

So, you finished your uninstall session and started to test your system when—all of sudden—your system won't boot. Of course, you are now in a state of total panic and you wonder why on earth you ever considered mess-ing with your system. Now, take a deep breath and relax. Things aren't as bad as they seem.

If you followed the uninstall procedures outlined in this book, you have a backup copy of your DOS configuration files—CONFIG.SYS and AUTOEXEC.BAT. All you need to do is to copy these backups into the root directory of your hard drive. To do this, follow these simple steps:

Tip

Always keep a backup copy of your original distribution disks for all of your applications, DOS, and Windows. These disks may be needed to restore your system if you have a problem with your system, Windows, or an application.

Tip
Be sure to always have a boot disk on hand. You can create a boot disk by formatting a blank floppy from File Manager. To create a boot disk, choose Disk, Make System Disk from the File Manager menu. You can then use that disk to boot your system from your A drive.

1. Load a boot floppy disk into your A drive. A boot floppy is a disk that has the bare essentials for booting your computer. If you don't have a boot floppy disk, you can use your DOS disks to boot your computer and restore DOS to its original state. If you don't have your original DOS disks or a boot floppy, go to a friend's computer and create a boot disk.

2. Once your system has booted from the floppy, you can copy the DOS configuration files to your root directory. Insert the floppy that contains the backup files and type the following at the DOS prompt:

   copy a:\autoexec.bat c:

   copy a:\config.sys c:

   This is assuming that the floppy containing the backups is in your A drive and your boot drive is C.

3. Remove the floppies from your hard drive and restart your computer.

4. At this point, your computer should boot as before. If you made any changes to the AUTOEXEC.BAT and CONFIG.SYS files during your uninstall session, you now know that one of the changes caused the problem. If you want to isolate the problem, use the EDIT command from DOS to view and edit the DOS configuration files, then restart your computer and see what happens.

5. If by some chance your system is still not booting up, you likely have a problem with some hardware in your system. Refer to your System User's Manual for troubleshooting information. The uninstall process usually doesn't change the CONFIG.SYS and AUTOEXEC.BAT files. However, these files are the only DOS-level files that, if changed, can cause problems when booting your system.

> **Note**
>
> If you deleted files from your system that are referenced in your DOS configuration files, you may get error messages when your system boots. However, these errors should not prevent your system from booting.

Windows Won't Start

You've just finished an uninstall session, rebooted your computer, and now Windows won't start. A likely cause of this is that an improper change has been made to the Windows configuration files, or a driver file that Windows needs to operate has been deleted. To get Windows up and running again, follow these steps:

1. Go to the WINDOWS directory using the DOS CD command and type **SETUP**. The Windows Setup program (a DOS-based setup routine) starts and lists the current drivers being used by Windows. Confirm the driver settings for the display, keyboard, mouse, and so forth. If any of these need to be changed, change them, and restart Windows. If everything is correct, go on to the next step.

2. Copy your backups of the SYSTEM.INI and WIN.INI files to the WINDOWS directory. To do this, go to the C:\ prompt and type the following:

    COPY A:*.INI C:\WINDOWS

    assuming that the backup files are on a floppy in your A drive and C:\WINDOWS is the directory that contains Windows.

    Start Windows. If Windows works, you know that a change in the .INI files caused the problem. If Windows still doesn't work, go to the next step.

3. You need to either reinstall Windows or restore your backup of the WINDOWS directory. If you have your installation disks, reinstall Windows first. If you can't reinstall Windows and get it to work, restore your WINDOWS directory using the backup of your WINDOWS directory (if you made one).

    If you have a backup of your entire system, you can select to restore either the WINDOWS directory or the entire system.

Your Application Won't Work

If an application won't work, you get some kind of error message that indicates the type of error. The most likely cause is a missing file or driver. It may also be the result of a modification to an initialization file. To correct this problem, simply reinstall the application that is having the problem. This will restore any missing files and restore the settings in the initialization files.

> **Note**
>
> Reinstalling an application does not affect your document files. They are not removed or overwritten.

Appendix B

Common UnInstaller Questions

UnInstaller is a very powerful utility with many features. This appendix contains many of the common questions that users have about how UnInstaller works and how to use UnInstaller to perform certain tasks.

I've installed and started UnInstaller. Now what do I do?

UnInstaller offers many features to help you maintain your system. What you do when you start UnInstaller depends on what you are trying to accomplish. This book presents a four-step uninstall process that you can use to uninstall applications and to clean up your system with UnInstaller 3.0. However, you don't have to follow this process to use UnInstaller.

Any feature in UnInstaller can be used independently. If you just want to free some disk space, for example, you can use the Windows Cleanup feature to locate and remove unnecessary files. If you want to delete an application, use the Delete Applications feature. If you are unsure about the best way to use UnInstaller, review the chapter that discusses the particular UnInstaller feature for additional guidelines.

I bought UnInstaller to remove applications. What are all the other features for?

There's more to maintaining your system and Windows than just deleting applications. You also need to remove unnecessary files and manage your system's configuration. Although UnInstaller's primary purpose is to delete applications, it provides additional features to help you keep your system clean and running smoothly.

Do I really need to back up my system before deleting applications and files with UnInstaller?

It's always a good idea to have a backup of your system before you make major changes like installing or uninstalling an application. With UnInstaller, however, it is not as important to have a backup. UnInstaller provides a Preferences section that allows you to enable backups for the Delete Applications, Duplicate File Finder, and Orphan Finder features. With backups enabled, you can restore any changes made to your system.

The Move Applications, Archive Applications, Transport Applications, INIClean, and Windows Cleanup features do not have backup options for the following reasons:

- A moved application can be restored by moving the application back to its original location.

- An archived application is a backup of an application. The original application is not deleted until the archive is created and confirmed.

- An application that has been transported is not removed or modified on the source system.

- INIClean and Windows Cleanup have their own backup capabilities.

What is SmartLinks and why is it important?

One of the hardest things to do when trying to delete an application is to determine what files are related to the application (.EXE) file. It is easy to identify files that are located in the application directory. However, application files can be found in several locations on your hard drive such as the WINDOWS or WINDOWS\SYSTEM directories. Files located in these directories may be shared by more than one application. SmartLinks was developed by MicroHelp to determine the interdependencies between applications and their files. SmartLinks uses intelligent processes to identify all the files that an application uses as well as to determine how many applications use each file. This way you can completely remove an application and all of its files without worrying about deleting a file that is being used by another application.

When I use the Delete Applications feature, my initialization files are modified automatically. Why do I need INIClean?

You are correct. Delete Applications does automatically update your initialization files. However, it only makes changes that relate to the application that you are removing. INIClean is useful for reviewing and editing any initialization file; the initialization file does not have to be associated with an application that you are removing. INIClean can help you modify entries, remove sections, edit associations, delete entire .INI files, and more.

I just ran out of room on my hard drive! How can I use UnInstaller to quickly free up some disk space without deleting any of my applications?

I suggest you start with Windows Cleanup. Windows Cleanup locates over a dozen different types of files that you can safely remove from your system. You can review these files and delete those that you don't use or need. To free up a lot of disk space fast, review your help files using Windows Cleanup. If you don't use the help file for an application, delete it. Help files are typically large and you can free up space quickly.

I am connected to a network and can't delete an application that I use on the network. What am I doing wrong?

You must be using the single-user version of UnInstaller. Only the network version of UnInstaller lets you modify and delete networked applications. However, some parts of the single-user version of UnInstaller recognize and access a network drive. For example, you can use a network drive as an intermediate location for a transported application.

I want to move an application from my office computer to my home computer. Can I do this with UnInstaller?

UnInstaller provides the Transport Applications feature to move an application, its files, and its settings to another computer. The Transport Applications feature makes an archive of an application that you can restore on another system. The application is restored onto the system with all settings and preferences intact. The original application is not modified or removed during the transport process.

Be aware of copyright violations when you are using Transport Applications. Read your software license agreement for product licensing information.

What is the difference between a backup and an archive with UnInstaller?

UnInstaller allows you to perform backups using most of its features. A backup file created by UnInstaller is really an archive of all the deleted files and modifications that were made by a particular feature. You can use the Restore feature to restore the changes stored in a backup. Restore retrieves the information from the backup and restores the system. Although a backup is a form of an archive, it is not the same as an archived application.

The Archive Applications feature creates an archive of an application, its files, and its settings. When UnInstaller archives an application, it takes everything that is related to the application, compresses it, and places it in an archive file. UnInstaller then replaces the application's icon with an archive application icon. To restore an archived application, simply double-click the archived icon.

In summary, a backup is really a safety net. You only use the backup file to restore a system when you have problems. An application is archived to save space on your hard drive with the intent that you will use the application in the future.

I have a lot of fonts installed on my system and I want to remove some of them. Do I need to go into the Control Panel to uninstall these fonts before I use Windows Cleanup to delete the font files?

No. Windows Cleanup automatically makes any of the required modifications to Windows when you choose to delete a font. If a font is registered with Windows, Windows Cleanup does everything necessary to remove the font file(s) from your hard drive and unregister the font in Windows.

What are orphaned files and why do I need Orphan Finder to find them?

Orphaned files are either Windows executable files that are not referenced in your Windows shell (Program Manager) or .DLL files that are not being used by any Windows executable file. Without an exhaustive search and comparison with Windows system information, it is extremely difficult to manually make all the comparisons required to identify orphaned files and to safely delete them. Orphan Finder uses SmartLinks technology and the Orphans Database to locate and identify orphaned files.

What happens if I use Windows Cleanup to delete the screensaver (.SCR) file that I am using with my Windows Desktop?

Windows Cleanup allows you to remove the screensaver file that is currently being used with the Windows Desktop. When the screensaver file is deleted, the appropriate settings are made in Windows and its initialization files to disable the screensaver feature.

I have located a lot of duplicate files using Duplicate File Finder. How do I know which duplicate files to delete?

Duplicate File Finder locates duplicate files and allows you to delete duplicates, leaving only one copy of a file. Duplicate File Finder offers several search options. If you are searching using the exact duplicate option, make sure that the file that remains is in a directory defined in the DOS PATH, in the WINDOWS directory, or in the WINDOWS\SYSTEM directory.

If you are searching using the duplicate filename option, delete the oldest file (assuming the files are just versions of the same file and not dissimilar files with the same name) and make sure the remaining file is in a directory defined in the DOS PATH, in the WINDOWS directory, or in the WINDOWS\SYSTEM directory.

What happens if I use Windows Cleanup to delete the wallpaper (.BMP) file that I am using with my Windows Desktop?

Windows Cleanup allows you to remove the wallpaper file that is currently being used with the Windows Desktop. When the wallpaper file is deleted, the appropriate settings are made in Windows and its initialization files to disable the wallpaper feature.

What is the Viewer and how can I use it?

The Viewer allows you to do many things. Its primary purpose is to allow you to view reports generated by UnInstaller. It also displays the contents of files or information about files (depending on the type of file). The way that you access the Viewer depends on the feature you are using. For example, double-clicking a filename using Windows Cleanup opens the Viewer so you can view the contents of the file. If you click the Viewer button on the UnInstaller toolbar, Viewer will be opened to allow you to view UnInstaller reports.

I've been using the Archive Applications feature to save disk space. Why don't I realize any disk space savings after archiving an application?

If you are using a disk compression utility such as DoubleSpace or Disk Doubler, you will not realize any disk space savings because the files have already been compressed. Archive Applications will attempt to compress the files, but will likely not be able to compress the files any further.

What is the difference between Move Applications and Transport Applications? They both seem to do the same thing.

Both features perform similar functions. Both copy an application, its files, and its settings to a new location. The difference, however, is the change in location. If you want to move an application to a new drive or directory on the same system, you need to use the Move Applications feature. To move an application to a different system, you need to use Transport Applications.

Appendix C

Removing Applications from Windows 95

Many people have been concerned about the introduction of Microsoft Windows 95. Windows 95 brings up many questions including those about uninstalling and the uninstaller utility market. Many believe that Windows 95 will eliminate the need for stand-alone uninstaller utilities; however, this is not true.

Guidelines for Uninstalling

Microsoft recently placed a new requirement on software manufacturers for use of the Windows 95 logo. All applications that use the logo on packaging must include an uninstalling utility that removes the application. On the surface, this seems like a good idea and in many ways it is. However, there are some problems with this philosophy.

As you learned in this book, uninstalling an application is a lengthy process. You need to weigh many factors before deleting certain types of files. If all uninstalling utilities produced by software manufacturers followed strict guidelines, Microsoft's uninstaller requirement would be a great idea. However, there are no guidelines and, inevitably, a poorly designed uninstalling utility will incorrectly remove a file or change a setting that keeps Windows or another application from working.

On the surface, it may seem like this couldn't happen. After all, the software manufacturer should know exactly what changes were made to the system when the application was installed. How could something go wrong? Let's look at an example.

Many Applications Share Files

Let's say you installed a new multimedia title. The multimedia title uses a runtime file for the application and a video driver for the videos. You install a second title that just happens to use the same runtime file and video driver. A few weeks later, you uninstall the first title using the provided uninstalling utility. It removes the files and changes made to the system including the runtime file and video driver. When you try to use the second title, it won't work! Why? Because the first title removed files needed by the second title.

Many applications use the same files whether these files are runtime files, .DLLs, or whatever. When an application is installed, it copies the file to the hard drive. If a file of the same name exists in the destination directory, it is overwritten. There are not two copies of the same file. If the file is deleted, it is no longer available to any application.

Most software manufacturers attempt to solve this problem by designing an uninstalling utility that will not remove questionable files from your system. The application will leave behind any file that may be used by another application. However, this creates a second problem: the application isn't really removed because it leaves files behind and, therefore, defeats the purpose of the uninstaller routine.

As a result, uninstalling methods (like those presented in this book) and uninstalling utilities like UnInstaller will still be needed with Windows 95 even with its significant changes and improvements.

Index

PLUG YOURSELF INTO...

THE MACMILLAN INFORMATION SUPERLIBRARY™

Free information and vast computer resources from the world's leading computer book publisher—online!

FIND THE BOOKS THAT ARE RIGHT FOR YOU!

A complete online catalog, plus sample chapters and tables of contents give you an in-depth look at *all* of our books, including hard-to-find titles. It's the best way to find the books you need!

- **STAY INFORMED** with the latest computer industry news through our online newsletter, press releases, and customized Information SuperLibrary Reports.

- **GET FAST ANSWERS** to your questions about MCP books and software.

- **VISIT** our online bookstore for the latest information and editions!

- **COMMUNICATE** with our expert authors through e-mail and conferences.

- **DOWNLOAD SOFTWARE** from the immense MCP library:
    - Source code and files from MCP books
    - The best shareware, freeware, and demos

- **DISCOVER HOT SPOTS** on other parts of the Internet.

- **WIN BOOKS** in ongoing contests and giveaways!

TO PLUG INTO MCP: → **WORLD WIDE WEB: http://www.mcp.com**

GOPHER: gopher.mcp.com

FTP: ftp.mcp.com